Revised and Ex

Instant
TAGALOG

PHRASEBOOK & DICTIONARY

How to Express Over 1,000 Different Ideas
With Just 100 Key Words and Phrases!

by Jan Tristan Gaspi and
Sining Maria Rosa L. Marfori

D0039779

TUTTLE Publishing
Tokyo | Rutland, Vermont | Singapore

Contents

Vowels

Tagalog is very simple to read as it is a phonetic language, where each letter has only one sound.

a like in <u>a</u>rt
e like in <u>e</u>nd
i like in <u>i</u>gloo
o like in <u>o</u>strich
u like in t<u>u</u>ne

Pronounce every letter even if they are repeated, making sure that each syllable is defined. When a word has multiple vowels, pronounce each letter separately.

maalaala (*ma-a-la-a-la* not *maa-laa-la*)
pakiusap (*pa-ki-u-sap* not *pa-kiyu-sap*)
uulit (*u-u-lit* not *uu-lit*)
iisip (*i-i-sip* not *ii-sip*)

Consonants

The Tagalog consonants are **b**, **d**, **k**, **g**, **h**, **l**, **m**, **n**, **p**, **r**, **s**, **t**, **w**, **y** and **ng**, representing the velar nasal. The consonants are unaspirated.

b like in <u>b</u>ack   voiced
k like the c in <u>c</u>abbage voiceless

d like in <u>d</u>og	voiced
g like in <u>g</u>ate	voiced
h like in <u>h</u>at	voiceless
l like in <u>l</u>ove	voiced
m like in <u>m</u>an	voiced
n like in <u>n</u>ut	voiced
ng like in so<u>ng</u>	voiced
p like in <u>p</u>ig	voiceless
r like in <u>r</u>at	voiced
s like in <u>s</u>nake	voiceless
t like in <u>t</u>in	voiceless
w like in <u>w</u>ag	voiced
y like in <u>y</u>acht	voiced

A voiced sound is when your vocal cords vibrate. A voiceless sound is when your vocal cords do not vibrate.

You will find that when two consonants are combined, the resulting sounds are similar to those in English.

dy like the j in jacket
ts like the ch in <u>ch</u>ocolate
sy like the sh in <u>sh</u>ow

Consonants **p**, **t** and **k**

In Tagalog, when the word's first syllable starts with the consonants **p**, **t**, **k**, you should pronounce the sound without a puff of air coming out of your mouth. Pronounce the letter **p** like the **p** in "part", **t** like the **t** in "star" and **k** like the **c** in "care".

Practice saying these words:
pangit *pa-ngit* ugly
payat *pa-yat* thin
pito *pi-to* seven
payong *pa-yong* umbrella
pera *pe-ra* money

tanong *ta-nong* question
tubig *tu-big* water
tasa *ta-sa* cup
tala *ta-la* star
takot *ta-kot* fear
tindahan *tin-da-han* store

kanan *ka-nan* right
kama *ka-ma* bed
kulay *ku-lay* color
kahit *ka-hit* even if
kaliwa *ka-li-wa* left
kaibigan *ka-i-bi-gan* friend

The Consonant **ng**

Some language learners find it difficult to produce this sound when it occurs in a word, especially when it occurs in the initial syllable of the word.

There are words that begin with **ng**. They should be pronounced similar to the **ng** in "long ago" or "sing along" when you blend the two words together.

Practice saying these words:
nga *nga* reiteration marker
ngayon *nga-yon* today
ngiti *ngi-ti* smile
ngunit *ngu-nit* but
ngipin *ngi-pin* tooth

There are words that have **ng** in the middle position. Pronounce them like you would for the words "singer" and "hanger" and not like "longer", "stronger" or "finger".

Practice saying these words:
pangalan *pa-nga-lan* (not *pang-ga-lan*) name
pangako *pa-nga-ko* (not *pang-ga-ko*) promise
bunga *bu-nga* (not *bung-ga*) fruit
kalinga *ka-li-nga* (not *ka-ling-ga*) care
pahinga *pa-hi-nga* (not *pa-hing-ga*) rest

On the other hand, words with **ng** + **g** at the middle are pronounced like "longer", "stronger" and "finger". Pronounce the velar nasal **ng** then the **g** sound.

Practice saying these words:
linggo *ling-go* week
pinggan *ping-gan* plate
langgam *lang-gam* ant
hanggang *hang-gang* until
tanggal *tang-gal* remove

The pronunciation of **mga** is *ma-nga*, and is read fast.
Ng as a stand alone is pronounced as *nang*.

Ito ang bahay ng pamilya ko.
I-to ang ba-hay nang pa-mil-ya ko.
This is my family's home. (lit. This is the house of my family.)

Kumain ang bata ng tanghalian.
Ku-main ang ba-ta nang tang-ha-li-an.
The child ate lunch.

Bumili siya ng mga gamit.
Bu-mi-li sha nang ma-nga ga-mit.
He/She bought some things.

Sentence Structure

The Filipino has two sentence structures, the **Subject + Predicate** (which describes the subject and contains a verb, i.e., "ate lunch") and **Predicate + Subject**. The **Subject + Predicate** follows the English sentence structure but is only used in formal writing and speech. This book focuses on the latter structure, **Predicate + Subject**, because it is used in everyday conversation. As you go further in this book, you will note that a common Filipino sentence would follow the **Verb + Subject + Object** order.

Filipino and Tagalog

Filipino is the national language of the Republic of the Philippines, but it is more popularly known in the world as Tagalog. It is the country's lingua franca and is based on Metro Manila Tagalog, with words borrowed and adapted from regional languages, dialects and foreign languages like Spanish, English, Chinese and Japanese.

The Philippines was colonized by the Spaniards for three centuries, the Americans for four decades, and the Japanese during the second World War. In addition to these colonizers, Philippines has traded with the Chinese, Arabs, Malays, and Indians since the pre-colonial period. Through the constant contact with these traders and also their colonizers, the Tagalog language has evolved, integrating and adapting some foreign words into its lexicon.

Tagalog is one of the Philippines' major languages along with Bikol, Ilocano, Ilonggo (Hiligaynon), Kapampangan, Pangasinan, Cebuano, and Waray (Samar-Leyte). These languages are represented by different regions: Ilocano and Pangasinan in Northern Luzon; Kapampangan in Central Luzon; Bicol in Southern Luzon; Cebuano, Ilonggo, and Waray in Visayas and Mindanao; and finally Tagalog in the densely populated National Capital Region and the Southern Tagalog Region in Luzon. Regardless, Filipinos across the country understand Tagalog.

Research and experience showed that the Tagalog's 20-letter **abakada** is inadequate for the writing requirements of a national language, thus eight letters (**C, F, J, Ñ, Q, V, X**, and **Z**) were added to the alphabet in 1987. These new letters represent sounds that are absent in Tagalog but present in the other native Filipino languages like Ivatan, Ibanag, Ifugao, Kiniray-a, Mëranaw and Bilaan. It is also then that "Pilipino" was replaced by the "Filipino language." These changes gave way to the faster modernization of the Filipino language.

Most of the borrowed/adapted words have been assimilated to Filipino. They are incorporated into native pronunciation and spelling according to the Filipino alphabet.

Spanish	Tagalog	Pronunciation	Meaning
cuarto	**kuwarto**	*ku-wart-to*	room
bicicleta	**bisikleta**	*bi-si-kle-ta*	bicycle
guapo	**guwapo**	*gu-wa-po*	handsome
carne	**karne**	*kar-ne*	meat
coche	**kotse**	*ko-che*	car
fiesta	**piyesta**	*pi-yes-ta*	feast
silla	**silya**	*sil-ya*	chair

English	Tagalog	Pronunciation
nurse	**nars**	*nars*
teacher	**titser**	*tit-ser*
tricycle	**traysikel**	*tray-si-kel*
computer	**kompyuter**	*kom-pyu-ter*
boxing	**boksing**	*bok-sing*
traffic	**trap-pik**	*tra-pik*
alcohol	**alkohol**	*al-ko-hol*

English words are also commonly used in the Tagalog language. They can either be paired as a **mag-*English word*** (see page 90 and 113) or on its own to form a sentence. When used on its own, this book will italicize the word.

Japanese	Tagalog	Pronunciation	Meaning
Jankenpon	**Jack en poy**	*Jack-en-poy*	Rock, Paper, Scissors
karaoke	**karaoke**	*ka-ra-o-ke*	A CD or machine stored with many songs with lyrics for people to sing along to
dandan	**dahan-dahan**	*da-han da-han*	gradually

The Basics

1 **Magandang Araw** Good Day!

Good morning
Magandang umaga
Magandang umaga often replaces the initial greeting of "Hi" or "Hello" in the morning, from 5:00am to 11:59am.

Good afternoon
Magandang tanghali
Tanghali, or "noon", starts exactly at 12:00pm and ends at 12:59pm. The word **tanghali**, when conjugated with **-an**, becomes **tanghalian**, meaning "lunch"; thus, 12:00 is considered as lunch time.

afternoon
Magandang hapon
The afternoon starts at 1:00pm and ends at 5:59pm.

Good evening/Good night
Magandang gabi
Evening starts at 6:00pm and ends at 11:59pm.

Tagalog uses linkers to link adjectives and nouns and to modify a noun. As a rule, if the adjective ends with a vowel, add **-ng**. If the adjective ends with a consonant, add **na**. Separate **na** from the adjective and the noun. In the examples above, we link **maganda** and **umaga**. Since **maganda** ends with a vowel, we attach the linker **-ng** to it.

Knowing the linkers will make studying the Filipino language a breeze. Use them when you want to describe something with adjectives and numbers.

2   **Kumusta/Kamusta** How are You?

How have you been?
Kumusta ka na/Kamusta ka na?

Good morning, how are you?
Magandang umaga, kumusta ka?

3   **Ka/Ikaw** You

Ikaw is used only at the start of the sentence.

Are you Jose?
Ikaw ba si Jose?

You are the prettiest (among the rest).
Ikaw ang pinakamaganda sa lahat!
See Intensives and the Superlative on page 114

all of you (plural of "you")
kayo
Although **kayo** is the plural form of **ka**, it is also a politer way to say "you", used to show respect to older people.

How are you?/How are you (formal)?
Kumusta ka?/Kumusta kayo?

4   **Ako** I

I am Filipino.
Pilipino ako.

I am Japanese.
Hapon ako.

I am American.
Amerikano ako.

_____ **ako**.
I am _____.

Briton British
Tsino Chinese
Pranses French
Italyano Italian
Koreyano Korean

5   Mabuti Good/Fine/Okay

I am fine.
Mabuti ako.

It is fine.
Mabuti lang.
An alternative to this is *Okay* **lang.**

6   Salamat Thank You

Many thanks/Thank you very much.
Maraming salamat.

Welcome. (lit., It is nothing.)
Walang anuman.
An alternative to this is **Ubos na.**

May can only be used in a sentence, not alone.

There is a taxi over there.
May taksi doon.

Is there a taxi over there?
May taksi ba doon?
Ba is the question particle. When placed after the first full word of a sentence, the sentence becomes a question.

There is. (I have).
Mayroon.
When asked a question that uses **may**, the positive response is **mayroon**.

Do you have money?/Do you still have money?
May pera ka ba?/May pera ka pa ba?

Yes there is.
Oo, mayroon.

Are you married?
May asawa ka ba?

I am married. Are you married?
Mayroon akong asawa. Ikaw mayroon ka bang asawa?

8 Wala None

It is gone.
Wala na.

There is nothing left.
Wala nang natitira.

(There is) no taxi.
Walang taksi.

There is no money changer at the airport.
Walang *money changer* sa *airport*.

free of charge/no payment needed
walang bayad

The airport transfer is complimentary.
Walang bayad ang *airport transfer*.

I am lost.
Nawawala ako.

I do not care.
Wala akong pakialam.

9 Tubig Water

Do you have (a glass of/bottled) water?
May tubig ba kayo?
It is generally understood that you are asking for drinking
water when using the word **tubig**.

I have (a glass of/bottled) water.
May tubig ako.

Is there (drinking) water in my room?
May tubig ba sa *room* ko?
Sa is the place marker and is equivalent to "in", "on", "at" and "with", and precedes a location or a place.

The water is gone.
Wala nang tubig.

There is no water left.
Wala nang tubig na natitira.

10 Pagkain Food

Do you have some food?/Do you have any food?
May pagkain ka?

I have (some) food with me.
May pagkain ako.

I do not have any food left.
Wala na akong pagkain.

Some Filipino dishes
Sinigang The signature sour soup of the Philippines. Pork and vegetables are boiled with tamarind until tender.
Adobo Pork and chicken cooked in soy sauce, vinegar and garlic
Tapsilog A meal composed of meat jerky, fried rice and fried egg

lechon roasted pork
baboy pork
manok chicken
baka beef
isda fish
gulay vegetable
prutas fruit

Arrival Notes

By now, you should have arrived at one of the three terminals of the Ninoy Aquino International Airport and have heard **Magandang umaga** or **Kumusta** from the crowd. The airport is near the cities of Paranaque and Pasay, two of the seventeen cities of Metro Manila. If you're not an adventurer ready to get lost in the city, but instead have been invited to the Philippines by a family or acquaintance, they will most likely be waiting for you at the arrival area.

Filipinos are known to be very hospitable. Your host will offer to pick you up and bring you to your hotel, prepare dinner arrangements etc., just to make sure you have what you need. It is genuine and sincere so there is no need to worry about returning the favor with a gift. This tradition of welcoming someone upon arrival is called **salubong**. In some instances, the entire family might welcome you at the airport, which gives you the opportunity to meet everyone and practice some of the basic phrases you have learned.

Whether you are the adventurer or someone who just experienced a **salubong**, the next part of the book will help you with the introductions as well as aid you in asking simple questions in Tagalog.

11 **Ano** What?

This word is often followed by **ang** and therefore becomes **anong**, which is short for **ano ang**.

What is this?
Ano ito?

What is that?
Ano iyan (*'yan*)**?**

What now?
Ano na?

What else?
Ano pa?

What is the Wi-Fi password?
Ano ang *WIFI password*?

12 **Ang/Si** The/Is

Ang is added before a subject or a common noun. It is used to mark the topic of the sentence. A similar marker is **si**, which is used with personal names, e.g., "Are you Adriana?" **Ikaw ba si Adriana?/Kayo po ba si Adriana?** To form the plural "are", use **mga** (*ma-nga*) after **ang**.

He/She is the host.
Siya (*Sha*) **ang *host*.**

This is the hotel.
Ito ang *hotel*.

There is no more water in the bottle.
Wala nang tubig ang bote.

Are you the tour guide?
Ikaw ba ang *tour guide*?/
Kayo po ba ang *tour guide*? (polite form)

Professions:
agent **ahente**
architect **arkitek**
dentist **dentista**
driver **drayber**
employee **empleyado**
engineer **inhinyero**
lawyer **abogado**
maid/helper **katulong**
seller **tindera**
soldier **sundalo**
author/writer **awtor**
veterinarian **beterinaryo**
student **estudyante** (*es-tu-jan-te*)

How do you say "I love you" in Tagalog?
Ano ang Tagalog ng (*nang*) **"*I love you*"?**

The Tagalog phrase for "I love you" is "**Mahal kita**".
Ang Tagalog ng "*I love you*" ay "Mahal kita".

What are your names?
Ano ang mga pangalan (*pa-nga-lan*) **ninyo?**

What are their names?
Ano ang mga pangalan nila?

We are Cher's friends.
Kami ang mga kaibigan *(ka-i-bi-gan)* **ni Cher.**

13   Noong/Sa In

Noong is a time marker indicating a past event or date, while **sa** indicates a future event or date.

last February
noong *February*

in 1997
noong 1997

in February/this coming February
sa *February*

in 2018
sa 2018

in the hotel
sa *hotel*

at the airport
sa *airport*

14 **Pangalan** Name

What is the name of the hotel?
Anong pangalan ng *hotel*?

What is the name of the driver?
Anong pangalan ng *driver*?

What is the name of this place?
Anong pangalan ng lugar na ito?

first name **unang pangalan**
last name/surname **apelyido**
nickname **palayaw**

15 **Ko** My
Namin/Natin Ours

My name is Joshua.
Joshua ang pangalan ko.

The name of my hotel is Manila Hotel.
Manila Hotel ang pangalan ng *hotel* ko.

My bottle has no more water.
Wala nang tubig ang bote ko.

Here is my passport.
Heto ang *passport* ko.

You are my only love.
Ikaw lang ang mahal ko.

What is our itinerary?
Anong *itinerary* natin?
Natin is used for statements that include the listener, while
namin excludes the listener.

Our favorite dishes are **adobo** and **sinigang**.
Adobo at sinigang ang paborito naming pagkain.

16 **Mo** Your (Singular)
Ninyo Your (Plural)

What is your favorite food?
Ano ang paborito mong pagkain?

Can I please see your passport?
Patingin ng *passport* mo?/
Patingin po ng *passport* ninyo? (polite form)

What is your name?
Ano ang pangalan mo?

What is your surname?
Ano ang apelyido mo?

What is your nickname?
Anong palayaw mo?

What is your address?
Anong *address* mo?

17 **Niya** *(Nya)* His/Hers
Nila Their

What is his/her name?
Ano ang pangalan niya?

Her name is Trisha.
Trisha ang pangalan niya.

They are Jodie and Robin.
Jodie at Robin ang pangalan nila.

Here are their passports.
Heto ang mga *passport* nila.

18 **Ni, Ng** *(Nang)* 's/Of

Ni or "of" and "'s" is the possessive marker for proper nouns and names, while **ng** is used for common nouns.

Jun is Cedric's father.
Tatay ni Cedric si Jun.

Grace is David's doctor.
Doktor ni David si Grace.

This is Mr. Song's passport.
Ito ang *passport* ni Mr. Song.

What is the name of Mr. Cruz's hotel?
Ano ang pangalan ng *hotel* ni Mr. Cruz?

19 **At** And

You and I
Ikaw at ako

Our names are Althea, Charice, and Mary Ann.
Althea, Charice, at Mary Ann ang mga pangalan namin.

Our favorite dishes are Bicol Express and **leche flan**.
Bicol Express at leche flan ang paborito naming pagkain.

20 **Taga-saan** (Where One Is) From

Taga-saan is used to ask one's place of origin. It is answered with **taga-** and the place one is originally from or where one lives.

Where are you from?
Taga-saan ka?

I am from the U.S.
Taga-U.S. ako.

I am from Makati.
Taga-Makati ako.

We are from the U.S.
Taga-U.S. kami.

Informal and Polite Introductions

Filipinos receive guests in a warm way, and will often go out of their way to make you feel at home. They will insist in showing you around or taking you out to dinner to try Filipino food.

Do not be offended if Filipinos ask too many personal questions. You might feel like you are being interrogated but it is just a way to get to know more about you. Asking your age and marital status are part of it. When asked "Why are you still single?" or "When are you going to get married?" do not feel obliged to respond directly, instead you can just laugh it off or give a response that you are comfortable with.

The words you just learned from the first two chapters will equip you in introducing yourself. You can now ask questions for basic information **Anong pangalan mo?**, **Taga-saan ka?**, **Kumusta ka?** "What is your name?", "Where are you from?", "How are you?" and answer them. Filipinos will be thrilled to hear you introduce yourself in Tagalog.

When addressing the elderly or superiors, it is customary to use the polite marker **po/ho** (interchangeable) to show respect or formality. The plural form of the pronoun **ka** is also replaced with **kayo**. You can say, **Kumusta po kayo?** You will notice that a lot of people use this form when talking to strangers, even if they are older than who they are talking to.

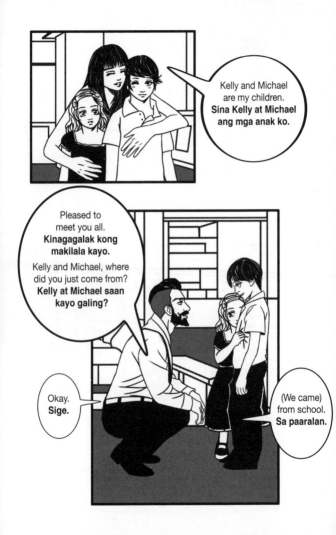

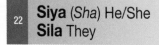

PART 3 Directions

21 Galing (Just) Come/Came From

I came from Japan.
Galing ako sa *Japan*.

I (just) came from Duty Free.
Galing ako sa *Duty Free.*

22 Siya (*Sha*) He/She
Sila They

He/she is the tour guide.
Siya ang *tour guide.*

He/she is my tour guide.
Siya ang *tour guide* ko.

She is Maria.
Siya si Maria.

They are your hosts.
Sila ang *hosts* mo.

lalaki male
babae female
bakla gay
lesbyan lesbian

asawa spouse/husband/wife
mga magulang parents

tatay father
nanay mother
pamilya family
anak child
mga anak children
anak na lalaki son
anak na babae daughter
kapatid sibling
mga kapatid siblings
kapatid na lalaki brother
kapatid na babae sister
pinsan cousin
tito uncle
tita aunt
lolo grandfather
lola grandmother
kasintahan boyfriend/girlfriend
kaibigan friend
kasama companion
binata single male
dalaga single female

He/She is my spouse.
Siya ang asawa ko.

They are my siblings.
Sila ang mga kapatid ko.

Pedro is my father and she is my mother.
Si Pedro ang tatay ko at siya ang nanay ko.

My father's name is Honesto.
Ang pangalan ng tatay ko ay Honesto.

23 **Kami** We (Excluding You) / **Tayo** We (Including You)

Are we officially a couple now?
Tayo na ba?
Tayo is used for statements that include the listener, while **kami** excludes the listener.

We are happy.
Masaya kami.

24 **Sige** Okay/All Right

Sige can be used as a term of agreement or to conclude a conversation and can also be used to plead.

Alright, let's go!
Sige, tara!

Pleeease.
Sige na.

Okay, I agree.
Sige na nga.

25 **Paalam** Goodbye

Okay, goodbye.
Sige, paalam.

Goodbye now.
Paalam na.

26 **Sino** Who

Who are you?
Sino ka?/Sino po sila? (polite form)

Who are they?
Sino sila?

Who is he/she?
Sino siya?

Who is that girl?
Sino ang babaeng iyan?

Who are your parents?
Sino ang mga magulang mo?

Who is with you?/Who is your companion?
Sino ang kasama mo?

Saan "where" is used when asking about an action.
To answer such a question, use **sa** + location/direction.
Nasaan "where" is used when asking about an object.
To answer such a question, use **nasa** + location/direction.
Nasa, similar to **sa**, means "in", "on" and "at".

Where did you (just) come from? The mall
Saan ka galing? Sa *mall*.

Where is the pick-up point? At the parking lot.
Nasaan ang sakayan? Nasa *parking lot*.

Where is the drop off point? At the mall's entrance.
Nasaan ang babaan? Nasa *entrance* ng *mall*.

Where is the restroom?/Where is the comfort room?
Nasaan ang *restroom*?/Nasaan ang C.R.?
Some Filipinos prefer using C.R. (comfort room) to refer
to the restroom.

On the basement (level).
Nasa *basement*.

Where are your companions?
Nasaan ang mga kasama mo?

Where is your family?
Nasaan ang pamilya mo?

Where is your husband/wife?
Nasaan ang asawa mo?

Where is my luggage?
Nasaan ang bagahe ko?

Where are they?
Nasaan sila?

mga lugar places
bangko bank
bahay house/ home
opisina office
palengke market
istasyon station
tindahan store
simbahan church
paaralan/eskuwelahan school
kainan eatery
restawran restaurant
ospital hospital
botika pharmacy
parke park
bundok mountain
tabing-dagat beach

harap front
likod back
itaas upstairs
ibaba downstairs

Note: One will observe that Filipinos have the habit of pursing their lips to point to an object. Sometimes, instead of using their forefinger, they will use their lips to point to a direction.

Nandito Over Here
Nandiyan Over There (Near)
Nandoon Over There (Far)

I am here at the hotel's entrance.
Nandito ako sa *entrance* ng *hotel*.

My taxi is already here.
Nandito na ang taksi ko.

I am already here.
Nandito na ako.

Pedro is over here.
Nandito si Pedro.

They are already here.
Nandito na sila.

They are over there.
Nandiyan sila.

My passport is there.
Nandiyan ang *passport* ko.

The restroom/comfort room is over there.
Nandoon ang C.R.

The restroom is on the 2nd floor.
Nasa *2nd floor* ang *restroom*.

I am upstairs.
Nasa itaas ako.

The Metro Rail Transit map is on page 5.
Nasa *page 5* ang mapa ng Metro Rail Transit.

I am in front of the train station.
Nasa harap ako ng istasyon ng tren.

Dito Here
Diyan There (Near)
Doon There (Far)

Just stay here.
Dito ka lang.

Just stay there.
Diyan ka lang.

Are you not going anywhere?/Are you just (waiting) there?
Diyan ka lang ba?

Mr. Marasigan's house is over there.
Diyan ang bahay ni Mr. Marasigan.

Who is single here?
Sino ang dalaga/binata dito?

The boys are over here and the girls are over there.
Dito ang mga lalaki at doon ang mga babae.

Diretso Straight
Kaliwa Left
Kanan Right

Just go straight.
Diretso ka lang.

(You) turn left here.
Kaliwa ka dito./Kaliwa po kayo dito. (polite form)

(You) turn right over there.
Kanan ka diyan.

The rest room is on the left/right.
Nasa kaliwa/kanan ang C.R.

31 **Paano** How/What is Going to Happen

How about you?/What is going to happen to you?
Paano ka?

How does this work?
Paano ba ito?

How about us?/What is going to happen to us?
Paano na tayo?

How do you get there?
Paano pumunta doon?

What is going to happen to your business in Australia?
Paano ang negosyo (*ne-go-sho*) **mo sa Australia?**

32 **Punta** Go

to go/went **pumunta**
going/go **pumupunta**
will go **pupunta**

Let us go there.
Pumunta tayo doon.

Go to the reception area.
Pumunta ka sa *reception area*.

How do you get there?
Paano pumunta doon?

How do I get to Manila?
Paano pumunta sa Manila?

How do I get to _____?
Paano pumunta sa _____?

I went to the embassy.
Pumunta ako sa embahada.

He/she went there.
Pumunta siya *(sha)* **diyan.**

I go to the gym in the morning.
Pumupunta ako sa *gym* **sa umaga.**

I will go to the money changer.
Pupunta ako sa *money changer*.

Mario will go to the beach in the afternoon.
Pupunta si Mario sa tabing-dagat sa hapon.

33 Lang Just

Just a moment.
Sandali lang.

Just here.
Dito lang.

Pull over here.
Dito na lang.

Pull over on the corner.
Dito na lang sa kanto.

Let's just stay over there.
Doon na lang tayo.

I will just go to the comfort room.
Pupunta lang ako sa *comfort room*.

It is just me here.
Ako lang ang nandito.

It is just you and me here.
Ikaw lang at ako ang nandito.

34 Malayo Far
Malapit Near

Is it far (from) here?
Malayo ba dito?

Is it nearby?
Malapit lang ba?

Is the _____ far?
Malayo ba ang _____?

Is the _____ nearby?
Malapit ba ang _____?

My hotel is just nearby.
Malapit lang ang *hotel* ko.
See Intensives and the Superlative on page 114

Where is the closest MRT/LRT station?
Saan ang pinakamalapit na estasyon ng MRT/LRT?
MRT = Metro Railway Transit
LRT = Light Railway Transit

35 Oo Yes
Hindi No/Not

I am no longer single (male).
Hindi na ako binata.

I am no longer single (female).
Hindi na ako dalaga.

I am not Filipino.
Hindi ako Pilipino.

Yes, I am going.
Oo, pupunta ako.

Yes, the pick-up point is far from here.
Oo, malayo ang sakayan.

Yes, I am married.
Oo, may asawa ako.

Never!
Hinding-hindi
Note: hindi is also used to negate sentences.

Not yet.
Hindi pa.

I do not understand you.
Hindi kita maintindihan.

The hotel is not far from here.
Hindi malayo ang *hotel*.

I am not going to the party.
Hindi ako pupunta sa *party*.

Street Food - Eat at Your Own Risk!

Now you have learned directions, as you roam around the busy streets of Manila or your chosen attractions, you may have noticed the presence of street food, which is everybody's comfort food. When you explore the streets, make sure you try these truly Filipino food.

Taho A popular Filipino snack usually sold in the morning by street vendors. It is made of soft fresh tofu with brown syrup and sago pearls.

Isaw Grilled skewered chicken/pork intestine

Kwek-kwek Boiled quail egg dipped in orange batter and deep fried in oil

Kikiam (*ki-kyam*) Deep fried pork and vegetable paste

Turon Thinly sliced bananas and a slice of **langka** or jackfruit rolled in a spring roll wrapper and fried in oil and a little brown sugar

Bananakyu/kamotekyu Skewered banana/sweet potato rolled in brown sugar and deep fried in oil

Balot Boiled duck embryo

Mangga at bagoong Green mangoes and shrimp paste

Sisig A popular Filipino appetizer comprising of chopped pig ears, face and liver, commonly served on a sizzling plate.
Bicol Express A famous dish in Bicol province. Pork slices and chilies are cooked in coconut milk.

36 Magkano How Much?

How much is the bill?
Magkano ang *bill*?

How much is the **balot**?
Magkano ang balot?

How much is the _____?
Magkano ang _____?

How much is my share?
Magkano ang *share* ko?

How much is the dollar exchange rate?
Magkano ang palitan ng dolyar?

37 Ito This
Iyan, Iyon (Yan, Yon) That

How much is this?
Magkano ito?

How much is that?
Magkano iyan?

This is Carl's bag.
Bag ito ni Carl.

This is Jodie's ticket and that is Althea's ticket.
Ito ang tiket ni Jodie at iyan ang tiket ni Althea.

Whose luggage is this?
Kanino ang bagahe na ito?

We can do this.
Kaya natin ito.

38 **Lahat** Everything/All

Everything is ready.
Handa na ang lahat.

Is everything here?
Nandito na ba ang lahat?

How much for everything?
Magkano lahat?

All of us.
Lahat tayo.

All of them.
Lahat sila.

Is everyone going?
Pupunta ba ang lahat?

They are all my siblings.
Mga *(ma-nga)* **kapatid ko silang lahat.**

---

39 **Numero** Number

mga numero numbers

1 **isa**
2 **dalawa**
3 **tatlo**
4 **apat**
5 **lima**
6 **anim**
7 **pito**
8 **walo**
9 **siyam** *(si-yam* or *sham)*
10 **sampu**
11 **labing-isa**
12 **labindalawa**
13 **labintatlo**
14 **labing-apat**
15 **labinlima**
16 **labing-anim**
17 **labimpito**
18 **labingwalo**
19 **labinsiyam** *(la-bin-si-yam* or *la-bin-sham)*
20 **dalawampu**
21 **dalawampu't isa**
22 **dalawampu't dalawa**
23 **dalawampu't tatlo**
30 **tatlumpu**
31 **tatlumpu't isa**
40 **apatnapu**

41 **apatnapu't isa**
50 **limampu**
51 **limampu't isa**
60 **animnapu**
61 **animnapu't isa**
70 **pitumpu**
71 **pitumpu't isa**
80 **walumpu**
81 **walumpu't isa**
90 **siyamnapu** (*sham-na-pu*)
91 **siyamnapu't isa** (*sham-na-put i-sa*)
100 **isang daan**
1,000 **isang libo**
1,000,000 **i-sang milyon**
Use the linkers **na** and **-ng** with numbers.

After 100 meters, turn right.
Pagkatapos ng isang daang metro kumanan ka.

How much is a kilogram and a half of pork?
Magkano ang isa at kalahating *kilo* ng baboy?

Paula is 28 years old.
Dalawampu't walong taong gulang si Paula.

I have a spouse and two children.
Mayroon akong asawa at dalawang anak.

There are six of us in the family.
Anim kami sa pamilya.

Pera Money
Bayad Payment
Sukli Change

magbayad to pay
nagbayad paid
nagbabayad pay/paying
magbabayad will pay

I have money.
May pera ako.

I do not have money.
Wala akong pera.

I do not have (any) money left.
Wala na akong pera.

(Here's) My payment.
Bayad ko.

Do I need to pay for this?
May bayad ba ito?

Let us just split the bill.
Hati na lang tayo sa bayad.

Where is my change?
Nasaan ang sukli ko?

I still have change.
May sukli pa ako.

Let us pay.
Magbayad na tayo.

Let me pay for everything.
Hayaan mo akong magbayad ng lahat.

Have you paid?
Nagbayad ka na?

Who paid (for it)?
Sino ang nagbayad?

How much? I will pay/It's my treat.
Magkano? Ako ang magbabayad.

pesos
piso

ten pesos
sampung piso

one hundred pesos
isang daang piso

41 **Piraso** Piece

6 pieces
Anim na piraso

How many pieces are in the box?
Ilang piraso ang nasa *box*?

42 **Ilan** How Many
Marami Many
Kaunti Few

How many pieces?
Ilang piraso?

How many are these?
Ilan ito?

How many of us are there?
Ilan tayo?

How many children do you have?
Ilan ang anak mo?

How many siblings do you have?
Ilan ang kapatid mo?

How long (in days) are you staying here?
Ilang araw ka dito?

How many months will you be staying here?
Ilang buwan ka dito?

43 **Bili** Buy

bumili to buy
bumili bought
bumibili buying/buy
bibili will buy

I bought food there.
Bumili ako ng pagkain doon.

I buy food from the grocery store.
Bumibili ako ng pagkain sa *grocery store*.

Where will you buy souvenirs?
Saan ka bibili ng *souvenirs*?

I am buying./Can I buy?
Pabili
The word **pabili** is used to get the attention of the seller, usually the street vendors.

I would like to buy _____.
Pabili ng _____.

I would like to buy a **taho**.
Pabili ng taho.

I would like to buy **balot**.
Pabili ng balot.

Malls and **Tiangge** in the Philippines

The Philippines houses three of the largest malls in the world, all located in Metro Manila: SM North EDSA, SM Megamall, and Mall of Asia, all located along the 24 km Epifanio Delo Santos Avenue, commonly known as EDSA. These malls have theaters, food courts, restaurants, grocery and clothing stores, bowling alleys, ice skating rinks, and local and international shops.

The Philippines is renowned for having big shopping malls that operate from 10:00am to 9:00pm. People come here not just to shop but also to meet friends, dine, and hold business meetings. The Mall of Asia has a convention center, arena, and concert grounds adjacent to it, while SM North EDSA has a skydome for events. The malls are also venues for mall tours of local singers, actors, and actresses. Considering the size of the malls, the variety of happenings, and the number of stores, Philippine malls have everything for everyone, thus "malling" is a part of Filipino culture.

Greenhills Shopping Center is known for being the place where you can get the lowest prices for the same items you will see in malls. It houses over 200 **tiangge** or small bazaar stalls in interconnected buildings. As you can haggle or **tawad** here, this is the best place to practice the phrases you learned in part 1 and 2, like **Magkano 'yan?** With this in mind, one should not hesitate to ask, **Wala bang tawad?** "Is there no discount?" Take note however that **tawad** is only applicable in **tiangge**, fruit stands, and **palengke**, or local markets.

Gusto Like or Want
Ayaw Do Not Like
Kailangan Need

Use the non-topic pronouns **ko**, **mo**, **niya** when you talk about **gusto**, **ayaw** and **kailangan**.

I'd like coffee.
Gusto ko ng kape.

I do not like this.
Ayaw ko ito.

I need Internet connection.
Kailangan ko ng *Internet connection*.

Would you like some water?
Gusto mo ba ng tubig?

I do not like alcohol.
Ayaw ko ng alak.

I'd like three pieces.
Gusto ko ng tatlong piraso.

Don't you like it?
Ayaw mo ba?

I need to go to Bonifacio Global City.
Kailangan ko pumunta sa Bonifacio Global City.

I want to go to a bar.
Gusto ko pumunta sa *bar*.

I don't like it there.
Ayaw ko diyan.

I need to buy water./I need water.
Kailangan ko bumili ng tubig./Kailangan ko ng tubig.

I want a lot.
Gusto ko nang marami.

I do not like it anymore./I do not want any more.
Ayaw ko na.

What do I need to bring?
Ano ang kailangan kong dalhin?

What do you want?
Anong gusto mo?

I just want some food.
Gusto ko lang ng kaunting pagkain.

I like this.
Gusto ko ito.

What do you need?
Anong kailangan mo?

I would like to rent a data SIM card/portable Wi-Fi router.
Gusto kong umupa ng *data SIM card/portable WiFi router*.

I do not like him/her.
Hindi ko siya gusto.

Use the infinitive form of the verb with **gusto**, **ayaw**, and **kailangan**: **Gusto/Ayaw/Kailangan** + **ko** + infinitive form of the verb

45 Kain Eat
Inom Drink

kumain to eat/ate
kumakain eating/eat
kakain will eat

uminom to drink/drank
umiinom drinking/drink
iinom will drink

Let us eat.
Kain tayo.

Let us drink.
Inom tayo.

I want to eat.
Gusto ko kumain.

I want to drink coffee.
Gusto ko uminom ng kape.

Have you eaten yet?
Kumain ka na ba?

Have you drunk water yet?
Uminom ka na ba ng tubig?

I do not want to eat cake.
Ayaw ko kumain ng *cake*.

I don't want to drink whiskey.
Ayaw ko uminom ng *whiskey*.

I ate at home.
Kumain ako sa bahay.

I had beer at the bar.
Uminom ako ng beer sa *bar*.

They are eating at the restaurant.
Kumakain sila sa restawran.

They are drinking.
Umiinom sila.

Where will we eat?
Saan tayo kakain?

Are you going to drink?
Iinom ka ba?

I do not eat meat.
Hindi ako kumakain ng karne.

I do not drink.
Hindi ako umiinom.

I want to eat **sisig**.
Gusto ko kumain ng sisig.

Let us have some (alcoholic) drinks later!/Let's drink later.
Uminom tayo mamaya!

Let us eat there.
Doon tayo kumain.

Do you drink?
Umiinom ka ba?

What do you want to eat?
Anong gusto mong kainin?

What drink are you having?
Anong gusto mong inumin?

---

46 **Dating** Arrive
Alis Leave

dumating arrived
dumadating arriving/arrive
dadating/darating will arrive

umalis to leave/left
umaalis leaving
aalis will leave

They have arrived.
Dumating na sila.

I need to leave.
Kailangan ko (na) umalis.

The guests (usually) arrive in the evening.
Dumadating ang mga *guests* ng gabi.

I have already left.
Umalis na ako.

I will arrive in the morning.
Dadating ako ng umaga.

Sorry, but I have to leave.
Pasensya na, kailangan ko nang umalis.

Will you be arriving (soon)?
Dadating ka ba?

I leave at 7:00 in the morning.
Umaalis ako ng 7:00 ng umaga.

I want to arrive there early.
Gusto ko dumating doon ng umaga.

Are you leaving (now)?
Aalis ka ba?

Are you still coming?
Dadating ka pa ba?

gawin to do
ginawa did
ginagawa doing
gagawin will do

What do you want to do?
Anong gusto mong gawin?

I need to do something tomorrow.
May kailangan akong gawin bukas.

What did you do yesterday?
Anong ginawa mo kahapon?

What are you doing?
Anong ginagawa mo?

Are you doing anything?
May ginagawa ka ba?

I am doing a lot of things./I am busy.
Marami akong ginagawa.

I am not doing anything.
Wala akong ginagawa.

What will you do tomorrow?
Anong gagawin mo bukas?

What will I do?/What do I do?
Anong gagawin ko?

48 **Uwi** Go Home

umuwi went home/to go home
umuuwi going
uuwi will go

Let's go home.
Uwi na tayo.

Go home.
Umuwi ka na.

I want to go home.
Gusto ko (na) umuwi.

I am going home tomorrow.
Uuwi na ako bukas.

49 **Sakay** Ride

sumakay rode/to ride
sumasakay riding/ride
sasakay will ride

I'd like to ride the jeepney.
Gusto ko sumakay ng jip.

Let's ride the bus.
Sumakay tayo ng bus.

Where does one catch the jeepney?
Saan ba sumasakay ng jip?

Catch the jeepney over there.
Doon ka sumakay ng jip.

I take the taxi in the morning everyday.
Sumasakay ako ng taksi sa umaga araw-araw.

What (means of transportation) are we taking?
Anong sasakyan natin?

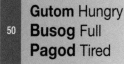

50
Gutom Hungry
Busog Full
Pagod Tired

I am hungry.
Gutom ako.

I am (already) hungry.
Gutom (na) ako.

Are you hungry?
Gutom ka ba?

I am full.
Busog ako.

I am still full.
Busog pa ako.

I am (already) tired.
Pagod (na) ako.

Are you tired?
Pagod ka na ba?

I am hungry and tired.
Gutom at pagod na ako.

High Context Communication

No group gathering will be complete without food. You would be perceived as a bad host if you do not have food. Filipinos have a communal culture and are known for their undying hospitality. Offering food is actually an alternative greeting. Filipinos are not comfortable taking a snack and relishing it alone. They will feel obligated to offer food and will often say **Kain tayo** or "Let us eat" or ask **Kumain ka na ba?** "Have you eaten yet?" because it is customary and polite.

The typical responses to these situations are to say "Go on/Do not mind me" which is **Sige lang**, "No, it is okay", **Hindi,** *okay* **lang**, first, then extend your appreciation for the offer by thanking them or saying **Salamat**.

While the food invitation may just be a simple, courteous gesture, if the person offering insists, you may want to give in to the request. Use your discretion to decide how much to take—if the person offering does not have a lot, then take a bit to refrain from offending or disrespecting them.

Remember, in the Philippines, like in most Asian cultures, people pay attention to facial expressions, along with the loudness and softness of the voice, and actions, and not just what is said, to decipher the speaker's true intention.

PART 6   Time Words

51   **Kailan** When?

When is your flight?
Kailan ang *flight* mo?

When did you arrive?
Kailan ka dumating?

When will you arrive?
Kailan ka dadating?

When are you leaving?
Kailan ka aalis?

When will we go to Cagayan?
Kailan tayo pupunta sa Cagayan?

When is the Sinulog Festival?
Kailan ang Sinulog Festival?

When is the best time to go to the Philippines?
Kailan ang pinakamagandang panahon pumunta sa Pilipinas?

Oras Time/Hour

What time is it?
Anong oras na?

What time are you leaving?
Anong oras ka aalis?

What time are you going home?
Anong oras ka uuwi?

What time is our flight?
Anong oras ang *flight* natin?

What time do you close?
Anong oras kayo nagsasara?

What time will you arrive?
Anong oras ka dadating?

How long?/How many hours?
Ilang oras?

2 hours
Dalawang oras

How long is the show?
Ilang oras ang palabas?

1 hour
isang oras

Note: Spanish numbers are usually used to express time.

Spanish Numbers
1 uno
2 dos
3 tres
4 kuwatro
5 singko
6 sais
7 siyete
8 otso
9 nuwebe
10 diyes
11 onse
12 dose
15 kinse
30 y medya
45 kwarenta y singko

____ o'clock
Alas-(Spanish number)
(An exception is 1:00, which is **ala-una** instead of **alas-uno**)

3:00 in the afternoon.
Alas-tres ng hapon.

It is 5:30.
Alas-singko y medya na.

It is 3:05.
Alas-tres y singko na.

Araw Day
Linggo Week

Lunes Monday
Martes Tuesday
Miyerkules Wednesday
Huwebes Thursday
Biyernes Friday
Sabado Saturday
Linggo Sunday/week

What day is today?/What day is that?
Anong araw ngayon?/Anong araw iyan?

Today is Friday.
Biyernes ngayon.

What day(s) are you available?
Anong araw ka *available*?

I am available on Saturday and Sunday.
***Available* ako sa Sabado at Linggo.**

I will arrive on Monday.
Sa Lunes ako dadating.

I am leaving on Sunday.
Aalis na ako sa Linggo.

I am leaving in a week.
Aalis na ako sa isang linggo.

I will be there for two weeks.
Dalawang linggo ako diyan.

We will be here in the Philippines for three weeks.
Tatlong linggo kami dito sa Pilipinas.

How many days will we be staying in this hotel?
Ilang araw ang *reservation* natin sa *hotel*?

54   **Buwan** Month/Moon
Taon Year

buwan-buwan monthly
taon-taon yearly

How long (in months) are you going to be in the Philippines?
Ilang buwan ka sa Pilipinas?

What month did you arrive?
Anong buwan ka dumating?

What month is the Chinese New Year?
Anong buwan ang Chinese New Year?

Which year was that?
Anong taon iyon?

How old are you?
Ilang taon ka na?

How many years did you live in Saudi Arabia?
Ilang taon ka tumira sa Saudi Arabia?

How old is the Rizal Park?
Ilang taon na ang Rizal Park?

I come to the Philippines every year.
Taon-taon ako pumupunta sa Pilipinas.

Months
Enero January
Pebrero February
Marso March
Abril April
Mayo May
Hunyo June
Hulyo July
Agosto August
Setyembre September
Oktubre October
Nobyembre November
Disyembre December
tuwing every

Christmas is in December.
Tuwing Disyembre ang Pasko.

The students' summer break is from March to June.
**Tuwing Marso hanggang Hunyo ang *summer break*
ng mga estudyante.**

I have a class every Monday and Wednesday.
May klase ako tuwing Lunes at Miyerkules.

My birthday is in May.
Bertdey ko sa Mayo.

Kanina Earlier
Ngayon Now
Mamaya Later (Today)

I ate earlier.
Kumain ako kanina.

I went to the mall earlier.
Pumunta ako sa *mall* kanina.

Right now!
Ngayon na!

Are we departing today?
Ngayon ba ang alis natin?

Are we leaving now?
Aalis na ba tayo ngayon?

What day is it today?/What is today?
Anong araw ngayon?

Mind that later.
Mamaya na iyan.

Where will you go later?
Saan ka pupunta mamaya?

What are you doing later?
Anong gagawin mo mamaya?

Is there something that you want to do tonight?
May gusto ka bang gawin mamayang gabi?

I will eat later.
Mamaya na ako kakain.

Kahapon Yesterday
Bukas Tomorrow

We arrived yesterday.
Dumating kami kahapon.

I had a meeting in the office yesterday.
May *meeting* **ako sa opisina kahapon.**

I bought some souvenirs at the store yesterday.
Bumili ako ng pasalubong sa tindahan kahapon.

I was busy yesterday./I did a lot of things yesterday.
Marami akong ginawa kahapon.

I will leave tomorrow.
Aalis na ako bukas.

My flight is tomorrow.
Bukas ang *flight* **ko.**

What will we do tomorrow?/What are we doing tomorrow?
Anong gagawin natin bukas?

I am not doing anything tomorrow.
Wala akong gagawin bukas.

Are you going tomorrow?
Pupunta ka ba bukas?

I will just go to the bank tomorrow.
Bukas na lang ako pupunta sa bangko.

57 Sundo Pick Up
Hatid Bring/Take to a Place

sunduin to pick up/pick up
sinundo picked up
sinusundo picking up/pick up
susunduin will pick up
susundo will pick up

ihatid to bring/take to a place
hinatid brought/took to a place
hinahatid bringing/taking to a place
ihahatid will bring/take to a place
maghahatid will bring/take to a place

Pick me up at the hotel.
Sunduin mo ako bukas sa *hotel*.

Take me to the airport.
Ihatid mo ako sa *airport*.

The guide picked me up from the hotel.
Sinundo ako ng guide sa *hotel*.

The taxi took me to Mrs. Lee's house.
Hinatid ako ng taksi sa bahay ni Mrs. Lee.

The van will pick me up at 6:00am.
Susunduin ako ng *van* ng 6:00am.

The van will take me to the airport.
Ihahatid ako ng *van* sa *airport*.

What time are you picking us up?
Anong oras mo kami susunduin?

What time are you taking me to the airport?
Anong oras mo ako ihahatid sa *airport*?

Who will pick us up at the airport?
Sino ang susundo sa amin sa *airport*?

Who will take me to the pier?
Sino ang maghahatid sa akin sa *pier*?

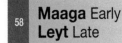

58   Maaga Early
Leyt Late

It is still early.
Maaga pa.

We will be leaving early tomorrow.
Maaga tayo aalis bukas.

Our flight arrived early.
Maaga dumating ang *flight* namin.

It's already late./You are late.
Leyt na./Leyt ka.

We are already late.
Leyt na tayo.

The bus will be arriving late.
Leyt dadating ang bus.

We are already late for the show.
Leyt na tayo sa palabas.

59 **Susunod** Next

Next time.
Sa susunod na lang.

the next day
sa susunod na araw

There is a feast next week.
May pista sa susunod na linggo.

I am going to Germany next year.
Pupunta ako sa Germany sa susunod na taon.

What is the next station?
Ano ang susunod na istasyon?

Where is the next stop?
Saan ang susunod na *stop*?

What do we do next?
Anong susunod nating gagawin?

Turn left on the next corner.
Kumaliwa ka sa susunod na kanto.

I will pay you next week.
Babayaran kita sa susunod na linggo.

Biyahe Trip
Bakasyon Vacation

When is the next trip?/What time is the next trip?
Kailan ang susunod na biyahe?/Anong oras ang susunod na biyahe?

When is your trip?
Kailan ang biyahe mo?

Is there a trip to Boracay today?
May biyahe ba sa Boracay ngayon?

I am on vacation.
Bakasyon ako ngayon.

When is your vacation?
Kailan ang bakasyon mo?

My vacation is next month.
Bakasyon ko na sa susunod na buwan.

transportasyon transportation
sasakyan vehicle
bisikleta bicycle
traysikel tricycle
bangka boat
barko ship
motor/**habal-habal** motorcycle
pedicab a small three-wheeled vehicle with attached bicycle that the driver pedals, also known as a cycle rickshaw or bike taxi.

bus bus
taksi taxi
tren train
kotse car
eroplano airplane

Filipino Time

You've received an invitation for a Filipino event that is scheduled to start at 5:00pm and are worried that you might not make it on time at the venue because of the traffic. Relax! Do not be surprised that upon arriving at 5:10pm, the event has yet not started—you might even be the earliest guest! This practice is commonly known as the Filipino Time, which is a later time (approximately 15 to 30 minutes) than what is scheduled.

Because of the outsourcing of businesses to the Philippines, more Filipinos have started to become disciplined to arrive on time for work, meetings and other appointments; thus, the practice of Filipino Time has diminished in professional and business-related situations. For informal events, such as parties held in the home, Filipino Time is still quite common.

Regardless of the type of event, being punctual will be greatly appreciated by the hosts. Not only does it guarantee you to not miss any part of the event, you will also have more time to mingle with the other guests.

PART 7 Verbs

61 **Puwede** May/Can

May (I) eat here?
Puwede ba kumain dito?

Can I buy tickets here?
Puwede ba bumili ng tiket dito?

Can I take a taxi over there?
Puwede ba sumakay ng taksi doon?

Are you free tomorrow?
Puwede ka ba bukas?

May I ride with you/in your car?
Puwede ba sumakay sa kotse mo?

Can you point me to the bus terminal?
Puwede mo ba ituro sa akin ang *terminal* ng bus?

Shall we date/become a couple?
Puwede ba maging tayo?

May I court you?
Puwede ba kitang ligawan?

May I hug/kiss you?
Puwede ba kitang yakapin/halikan?

May I accompany you?
Puwede ba kitang samahan?

May I borrow your phone?
Puwede ko ba mahiram ang telepono mo?

Can I buy you a drink?
Puwede ba kitang ibili ng inumin?

Yes, you can/may.
Oo, puwede.

Not possible/ (you) cannot/(you) may not.
Hindi puwede.

Not everyone can go tomorrow.
Hindi lahat puwede pumunta bukas.

May I add you on Facebook/Instagram/Snapchat?
Puwede ba kitang i-*add* sa *Facebook/Instagram/ Snapchat*?

Can we take a picture together?
Puwede ba tayong magpa-*picture* na magkasama?

62 Kita See

makita to see
nakita saw
nakikita seeing/see
makikita will see

I want to see you.
Gusto kita makita.

Can I see the bus schedule?
Puwede makita ang *schedule* ng biyahe ng bus?

I have seen that.
Nakita ko na iyan.

I have seen the show.
Nakita ko na ang palabas.

I saw him/her yesterday.
Nakita ko siya kahapon.

Can you see the show?
Nakikita mo ba ang palabas?

I will see Mrs. Santos tomorrow.
Makikita ko si Mrs. Santos bukas.

You will see, the place is really beautiful.
Makikita mo, maganda talaga ang lugar.

63 **Magkita** Meet Up

magkita to meet up
nagkita met up
nagkikita meeting up/meet up
magkikita will meet up

Let us meet on Saturday.
Magkita tayo sa Sabado.

Let us meet up at the Luneta Park parking lot.
Magkita tayo sa *parking lot* ng Luneta Park.

When can we see each other again?
Kailan tayo puwedeng magkita ulit?

Do you want to meet up?
Gusto mo magkita tayo?

We met at the restaurant yesterday.
Nagkita kami kahapon sa restawran.

What time shall we meet?
Anong oras tayo magkikita?

Where shall we meet tomorrow?
Saan tayo magkikita bukas?

When are we going to meet again?
Kailan tayo ulit magkikita?

Will we still meet up/see each other?
Magkikita pa ba tayo?

64 Kasi/Dahil Because

I went home because I am tired.
Umuwi na ako kasi pagod na ako.

I am late because my car broke down.
Leyt ako kasi nasira ang kotse ko.

I am hungry because I did not eat earlier.
Gutom ako kasi hindi ako kumain kanina.

We will meet up at John's house because it is his birthday.
Magkikita kami sa bahay ni John kasi bertdey niya.

Can I ask for (some) money because I (just) got robbed?
Puwedeng pautang, nanakawan kasi ako?

I cannot leave you, because I love you.
Hindi kita puwedeng iwan dahil mahal kita.

I want to go to Boracay because of (to see) its white sand.
Gusto ko pumunta sa Boracay dahil sa puting buhangin.

65 Akyat Go Up
Baba Go Down

umakyat to go up/went up
umaaakyat go up/going up
aakyat will go up

bumaba to go down/went down
bumababa go down/going down
bababa will go down

I want to go up the mountain.
Gusto ko umakyat ng bundok.

I do not want to go down.
Ayaw ko bumaba.

I need to go up to my room.
Kailangan ko umakyat sa *room* ko.

We need to head down (the mountain) now because it is getting late (in the evening).
Kailangan na natin bumaba (ng bundok) kasi gabi na.

66   **Papunta** Going To/En Route/Headed To

Are you on your way?
Papunta ka na ba?

We are on our way there.
Papunta na kami diyan.

I am heading there now./I am on my way there.
Papunta na ako diyan.

He/She is headed to Davao tomorrow afternoon.
Papunta siya sa Davao bukas ng tanghali.

Tomorrow is my trip to Manila.
Bukas ang biyahe ko papuntang Manila.

Is this the way to the church?
Ito ba ang papunta sa simbahan?

Where is this headed?
Saan ito papunta?

Where is the bus that leaves at 1:00pm headed to?
Saan papunta ang bus na aalis mamayang 1:00pm?

67   **Lakad** Walk   **Takbo** Run

maglakad to walk
naglakad walked
naglalakad walk/walking
maglalakad will walk

tumakbo to run/ran
tumatakbo run/running
tatakbo will run

Let's walk.
Maglakad tayo.

I want to walk.
Gusto ko maglakad.

I will walk to the mall.
Maglalakad ako papunta sa *mall*.

(You) run.
Tumakbo ka.

We will run/jog later.
Tatakbo kami mamaya.

He ran to his office because he was going to be late.
Tumakbo siya papunta sa opisina kasi leyt na siya.

I am tired, I do not want to walk.
Pagod na ako, ayaw ko nang maglakad.

68 Pahinga Rest

magpahinga to rest
nagpahinga rested
nagpapahinga rest/resting
magpapahinga will rest

I need to rest now./I need to rest.
Kailangan ko nang magpahinga./Kailangan ko magpahinga.

I just took a rest yesterday.
Nagpahinga lang ako kahapon.

I took a rest from work and went to the beach.
Nagpahinga ako sa trabaho at pumunta sa tabing-dagat.

I am resting right now.
Nagpapahinga ako ngayon.

We will rest (take a break) tomorrow.
Magpapahinga kami bukas.

69 Gising Awake

gumising to wake up/woke up
gumigising wake up
gigising will wake up
gisingin to be woken up

Are you still up/awake?
Gising ka pa ba?

Wake up!
Gumising ka na!

I need to wake up early tomorrow.
Kailangan ko gumising nang maaga bukas.

I will wake up later at noon.
Gigising ako mamayang tanghali.

Wake me up later.
Gisingin mo ako mamaya.

I will wake up early tomorrow because my flight is at 5:00.
Maaga ako gigising bukas dahil 5:00 ang *flight* ko.

I will wake up late tomorrow so I can get drunk tonight.
Leyt ako gigising bukas dahil maglalasing ako mamayang gabi.

⌐70 Tulog Asleep

matulog to sleep
natulog slept
natutulog sleep/sleeping
matutulog will sleep
nakatulog able to sleep

They are asleep.
Tulog na sila.

Paolo and Jann are already asleep.
Tulog na sina Paolo at Jann.

Go to sleep.
Matulog ka na.

Let us go to sleep.
Matulog na tayo.

I am going to sleep.
Matutulog na ako.

What time will you go to sleep?
Anong oras ka matutulog?

I will go to sleep at 12:00pm.
Matutulog ako mamayang alas-dose.

I went to sleep early.
Natulog ako nang maaga.

Were you able to sleep?
Nakatulog ka ba?

I could not sleep in the plane.
Hindi ako nakatulog sa eroplano.

My sleep last night was horrible. I kept waking up.
Ang pangit ng tulog ko kagabi, gising ako nang gising.

Learning the Verbs and Affixes

It can be a daunting task to learn when to use an affix with a verb. The best way to learn this is to remember the words, phrases and sentences and to become comfortable in sentence construction.

Constructing and saying a sentence at the very moment when you are recalling, doing, and planning about an action is a great way to remember the right usage of an affix with a verb. This would be greatly useful for verbs that are used every day such as, wake up, eat, drink, leave, walk, read, write, arrive, shower, and sleep.

Let us take "to eat" as an example. While eating your lunch, say, **Kumakain ako ng isda**, "I am eating fish". Follow this with a recollection of what you ate for breakfast, **Kumain ako ng itlog**, "I ate egg". Finally, start planning on what to eat for dinner by saying, **Kakain ako ng spaghetti**, "I will eat spaghetti". You just learned the past, present, and future form of the infinitive **kain**, "to eat". Try doing this routine with the other nine verbs mentioned in this chapter for a week until it becomes second nature.

Once you have mastered the basic structure of Verb + Subject + Object, you can start making your sentences more complex by adding time.

I am eating fish right now.
Kumakain ako ng isda ngayon.

I ate an egg earlier this morning.
Kumain ako ng itlog kaninang umaga.

I will eat spaghetti tonight.
Kakain ako ng *spaghetti* mamayang gabi.

Once you get into a habit of learning Tagalog verbs this way, you will be surprised how many words you have learned and how quickly you have learned to construct sentences within a week.

PART 8 Adjectives

71 Kulay Color

pula red
puti white
berde green
dilaw yellow
asul blue
itim black
kulay ube purple
kahel orange

What is your favorite color?/What color do you like?
Ano ang paborito mong kulay?/Anong kulay ang gusto mo?

What colors are available?
Anong mga kulay ang mayroon?

I want a yellow bag.
Gusto ko ng dilaw na *bag*.

Do you have any other color?
May ibang kulay ka pa ba?

Do you have a red dress?
May pulang damit ba kayo?

How much are the white shoes?
Magkano ang puting sapatos?

Do you have a darker/lighter color?
May mas *dark/light* kayo na kulay?

mga damit clothes
blusa blouse
polo polo shirt
pantalon jeans
damit dress
palda skirt
sapatos shoes
medyas socks
sumbrero hat

72 | **Maganda** Beautiful
Pangit Ugly/Bad

She is pretty!
Maganda siya!

This is pretty.
Maganda ito.

Is (it) pretty?/Is (she) pretty?
Maganda ba?

Your blouse is pretty.
Maganda ang blusa mo.

This is ugly.
Pangit ito.

Is it ugly?
Pangit ba?

The view from our hotel room is bad.
Pangit ang *view* ng *hotel room* namin.

The service here is bad.
Pangit ang *service* dito.

Try to use **Hindi masyado** "not very" instead of "bad". Thus, you would say "The view from our hotel room is not very good" or **Hindi masyado maganda ang *view* ng *hotel room* namin.**

73 Masyado Too/Very

Masyado is used to intensify an adjective.

Sagada is very far away.
Masyadong malayo ang Sagada.

Too expensive!
Masyadong mahal!

It is too early.
Masyadong maaga.

The bus departure (time) is too early.
Masyadong maaga ang alis ng bus.

The _____ is too expensive!
Masyadong mahal ang _____!

You are too much!
Masyado ka naman!

74 **Malinis** Clean
Madumi Dirty

Is this water clean?
Malinis ba ang tubig na ito?

The room is clean and pretty.
Malinis at maganda ang *room*.

That water is not clean, buy bottled water.
Hindi malinis ang tubig na iyan, bumili ka ng *bottled water*.

My room is very dirty.
Masyadong madumi ang *room* ko.

75 **Maingay** Noisy
Tahimik Quiet

Room 506 is noisy.
Maingay ang *room* 506.

It is too noisy in here.
Masyadong maingay dito.

It is quiet in here.
Tahimik dito.

It is quiet in the church.
Tahimik sa simbahan.

I want to rest in a quiet place.
Gusto ko magpahinga sa tahimik na lugar.

76

Malaki Big
Maliit Small

Is this too big/small for me?
Malaki/maliit ba masyado ito para sa akin?

Do you have this in a bigger/smaller size?
May malaki/maliit ba kayo nito?

Too big/small.
Masyadong malaki/maliit.

I want a big room./I would like a big room.
Gusto ko ng malaking *room*.

The bed is too small.
Masyadong maliit ang kama.

The dress is too big.
Masyadong malaki ang damit.

77

Mababaw Shallow
Malalim Deep

The hotel's swimming pool is shallow.
Mababaw ang *swimming pool* sa *hotel*.

The beach's water is too shallow.
Masyadong mababaw ang tubig sa tabing-dagat.

Is it deep?
Malalim ba?

It is shallow.
Mababaw lang.

It is deep over there.
Malalim diyan.

78   **Mura** Cheap/Affordable
Ma-hal Expensive

Is it cheap/expensive over there?
Mura/mahal ba doon?

The clothes in Greenhills are sold at a cheap price.
Mura lang ang mga damit sa Greenhills.

The food in the fast food (restaurant) is affordable.
Mura ang pagkain sa *fast food*.

The food in the hotel is very expensive.
Masyadong mahal ang pagkain sa *hotel*.

So expensive! No discount?
Ang mahal naman! Wala bang tawad?

79   **Malamig** Cold
Mainit Hot

It is cold today.
Malamig ngayon.

The water is cold.
Malamig ang tubig.

Do you have cold water (ice water)?
May malamig na tubig ba kayo?

I would like a (glass of) cold water.
Gusto ko ng malamig na tubig.

It is hot in here.
Mainit dito.

It is too hot.
Mainit masyado.

I do not like hot coffee.
Ayaw ko ng mainit na kape.

80 Masarap Delicious/Tasty/Good

Is it delicious? Is that good/tasty?
Masarap ba?/Masarap ba iyan?

Do they serve good food there?
Masarap ba ang pagkain doon?

The food in the restaurant is good.
Masarap ang pagkain sa restawran.

The food is not good.
Hindi masarap ang pagkain.

Where can we eat good food?
Saan masarap kumain?

The _____ is delicious.
Masarap ang _____.

lasa taste
matamis sweet
maasim sour
maalat salty
maanghang spicy

What does it taste like?
Anong lasa?

How does the food taste?
Kumusta ang lasa ng pagkain?

Do you eat spicy food?
Kumakain ka ba ng maanghang na pagkain?

I do not like (food that is) too spicy/sweet.
Ayaw ko ng masyadong maanghang/matamis.

The cake is too sweet.
Masyadong matamis ang keyk.

I like sweet/sour/salty/spicy food.
**Gusto ko ng matamis/maasim/maalat/maanghang
na pagkain.**

The Power of Affixes

Studying Tagalog can be fun and yet also frustrating.

The language is abundant in affixes, with prefixes,
infixes and suffixes. Multiple affixes can even be

attached to roots or simple words all at the same time. The affixes play a great role in the morphology of Filipino language but one cannot see the full picture unless these are related to the roles they assume when they occur in sentences" (Cubar and Cubar 1994:37).

For example, the word **ganda** "beauty" can be used with
ma + **ganda** beautiful
You look beautiful in that dress.
Maganda ka sa suot mong iyan.

g + **um** + **anda** to become beautiful
That's a flattering color on you.
Gumanda ka lalo sa kulay ng suot mo.

ganda + **han** beautify/improve
Brighten up your smile later./(lit., Do your best and put on your prettiest smile.)
Gandahan mo ang ngiti mo mamaya.

pampa + **ganda** something to make something beautiful
Bring makeup tonight (to make yourself prettier).
Magdala ka ng pampaganda mamayang gabi.

ka + **ganda** + **han** beauty
I have fallen in love with her beauty.
Nakaka-*in love* ang kagandahan niya.

sing + **ganda** as beautiful as
You look as pretty as Jessica Alba in that outfit.
Sa suot mong iyan sing-ganda mo na si Jessica Alba.

PART 9

Conjunctions

81 **O** Or

Yes or no?
Oo o hindi?

Are we going or not?
Pupunta ba tayo o hindi?

Do you like it or not?
Gusto mo ba o ayaw mo?

Are you hungry or (are you) already full?
Gutom ka pa ba o busog na?

Is the mango sour or sweet?
Maasim ba o matamis ang mangga?

Do you want hot or cold coffee?
Gusto mo ba ng mainit o malamig na kape?

What color t-shirt do you want, white or black?
Anong kulay ang gusto mong *t-shirt*, puti o itim?

What do you want, **sinigang** or **adobo**?
Ano ang gusto mo, sinigang o adobo?

Where do you all want to go on Saturday, Boracay
or Palawan?
**Saan ninyo gusto pumunta sa Sabado, sa Boracay
o Palawan?**

When do you all want to go the beach, in the morning or at night?
Kailan ninyo gusto pumunta sa tabing-dagat, sa umaga o sa gabi?

Do you love me or not?
Mahal mo ba ako o hindi?

Is it true or not?
Totoo ba o hindi?

Which one do you like, this or that?
Alin ang gusto mo, ito o iyan?

Let us keep in touch by WhatsApp or Line.
Mag-usap tayo sa *WhatsApp* o *Line*.

82 **At** And

He/she ate and left the house.
Kumain siya at umalis sa bahay.
At can also be used to compound sentences.

I picked him/her up and we went to the hospital.
Sinundo ko siya at pumunta kami sa ospital.

We want to go to the Banaue Rice Terraces and see the rice fields.
Gusto namin pumunta sa Banaue Rice Terraces at makita ang mga palayan.

I am tired and he/she is hungry.
Pagod na ako at nagugutom siya.

Pero But

I have already eaten but I am still hungry.
Kumain na ako pero gutom pa rin ako.

I want to hike to the peak of Mt. Apo, but it is too far (away).
Gusto ko umakyat sa tuktok ng Mt. Apo pero ang layo.

I want to buy fishball(s) but I do not have change.
Gusto ko bumili ng fishball pero wala akong barya.

I want to go out but it is still raining heavily (lit. hard).
Gusto ko lumabas pero malakas pa ang ulan.

Thank you for the offer, but I have already eaten.
Salamat sa alok pero kumain na ako.

I am okay now, but it still hurts.
Okay na ako, pero masakit pa rin.

I want to go, but I am really tired.
Gusto ko pumunta, pero pagod na ako.

Para So That

Let us leave early so that we will not be late.
Umalis tayo nang maaga para hindi tayo ma-leyt.

Come here so we can see each other.
Pumunta ka dito para magkita tayo.

I will go to the mall to buy some souvenirs.
Pupunta ako sa *mall* para bumili ng mga pasalubong.

I want to go to Cebu so I can celebrate the Sinulog Festival.
Gusto ko pumunta sa Cebu para magdiwang ng Sinulog Festival.

Para states the purpose and is often paired with **maka** (**para** + **maka**) to mean "to be able to" or "can" when attached to a verb.

I will rest right now so that I can go to the club tonight.
Magpapahinga ako ngayon para makapunta ako mamayang gabi sa *club*.

Go to sleep now, so that you can wake up early tomorrow.
Matulog ka na para makagising ka nang maaga bukas.

What do I need to take to get around Manila?/What do I need to ride so that I can get around Manila? (lit.)
Ano ang kailangan kong sakyan para maka-ikot ako sa Manila?

85 Kaya That is Why/So

I have an early flight tomorrow, so I need to sleep now.
Maaga ang *flight* ko bukas kaya kailangan ko nang matulog ngayon.

The restaurant was expensive and had small servings. That is why we just decided to eat street food.
Mahal at kaunti ang *servings* sa restawran kaya kumain na lang kami ng *street food*.

My flight was delayed so I've arrived in Manila late.
Delayed ang *flight* ko kaya leyt ang pagdating ko sa Manila.

The clothes are cheap. That is why I bought a lot.
Mura ang mga damit kaya bumili ako nang marami.

There was a bad traffic jam, so we just walked.
Trapik kaya naglakad na lang kami.

The traffic in Manila is really bad, so I need to leave home early tomorrow.
Masyadong trapik sa Manila, kaya kailangan kong maaga umalis bukas sa bahay.

86 **Tapos** Then/And Then

Turn right, then turn left, and then go straight.
Kumanan ka, tapos kumaliwa ka, tapos dumiretso ka.

Let us go to the mall, then to the movie theater, and then to the food court.
Pumunta tayo sa *mall*, tapos sa *movie theater*, tapos sa *food court*.

We went up (hiked) the Mayon Volcano, then we ate Bicol Express in Naga City.
Umakyat kami sa Mayon Volcano, tapos, kumain kami ng Bicol Express sa Naga City.

I like that better.
Mas gusto ko iyan.

What/which do you like better?
Ano ang mas gusto mo?

Do you like this better than this one/that one?
Mas gusto mo ba ito kaysa dito/diyan?

I want something bigger than this.
Gusto ko ng mas malaki pa rito.

It is hotter in the Philippines than in California.
Mas mainit sa Pilipinas kaysa sa.

The items in Greenhills are more expensive than in
Ayala Malls.
**Mas mahal ang bilihin sa Greenhills kaysa sa
Ayala Malls.**

Do you have a bigger size?
Mayroon ba kayo na mas malaking *size*?

It takes longer to take a taxi than to walk to get to the
mall because of traffic.
**Mas matagal ang mag-taksi kaysa sa maglakad
papunta sa *mall* dahil sa trapik.**

The souvenirs here are cheaper than the ones downtown.
Mas mura ang mga pasalubong dito kaysa sa sentro.

The seafood in Coron, Palawan is cheaper and fresher than those in Manila.
Mas mura at sariwa ang mga *seafoods* sa Coron, Palawan kaysa sa Manila.

88　Paki... Please

Please say that again./Please repeat.
Paki-ulit.
"Please" usually precedes a verb.

Please bring me to the hotel.
Pakihatid ako sa *hotel*.

Please pick me up at 3:00pm.
Pakisundo ako ng 3:00pm.

Please charge it to my credit card.
Paki-*charge* sa *credit card* ko.

Please translate this to English.
Paki-*translate* ito sa *English*.

Can you please say that again?
Puwede paki-ulit ang sinabi mo?

Can you please slow down?
Puwede pakibagalan?

Can you please hand me the _____?
Paki-abot ang _____?

Naka Was/Were Able To/Could

I was able to go to Bohol and Cebu.
Nakapunta ako sa Bohol at Cebu.

We were not able to go/make it.
Hindi kami nakapunta.

Were you able to eat/try some Filipino food?
Nakakain ka ba ng mga pagkaing Pilipino?

I was able to try/eat **balot**.
Nakakain ako ng balot.

We were able to make it to the airport on time.
Nakarating kami sa *airport* sa oras.

I was not able to make it on time.
Hindi ako nakarating sa oras.

We were able to buy souvenirs at Greenhills Shopping Center.
Nakabili kami ng mga pasalubong sa Greenhills Shopping Center.

I was not able to buy souvenirs because I did not have enough time.
Hindi ako nakabili ng mga pasalubong dahil kulang sa oras.

Mag-(English Word)
Making English Words Into Filipino Words

(infinitive) **mag** + English word
(past) **nag** + English word
(present) **nag**+ first syllable of English word + English word
(future) **mag** + first syllable of English word + English word

Let us meet tomorrow.
Mag-*meeting* tayo bukas.

Let us have lunch in Jollibee.
Mag-*lunch* tayo sa Jollibee.

I booked a ticket going to Ilocos.
Nag-*book* ako ng *ticket* papunta sa Ilocos.

We met in the mall.
Nag-*meet* kami sa *mall*.

He/ she works in Quezon City.
Nagwo-*work* siya sa Quezon City.

They are reviewing (revising) for the exam.
Nagre-*review* sila para sa eksam.

I will go online tonight.
Mag-o-*online* ako mamayang gabi.

I will just take the bus.
Magbu-bus na lang ako.

I will order some food first.
Mag-o-*order* na ako ng pagkain.

It was raining outside so we just stayed at home.
Maulan sa labas kaya nag-*stay* na lang kami sa bahay.

I want to go shopping, but I do not have any money left.
Gusto ko mag-*shopping* pero wala na akong pera.

Intensives and the Superlative

By now you should have learned several adjectives to describe your feelings and surroundings. You can now say that "the place is beautiful" or **Maganda ang lugar!** Should **maganda** be inadequate to express your amazement at the beauty of the nature and attractions found in the Philippines, using a more intense form of the adjective can help convey your delight. There are several ways to intensify this sentence, such as **Ang ganda ng lugar**, **napakaganda ng lugar** or **Ang ganda-ganda ng lugar**.

Simple
The Philippines is beautiful.
Maganda ang Pilipinas.

Using mas- (more/-er) for unequal comparison
The Philippines is more beautiful.
Mas maganda ang Pilipinas.

Using the superlative form pinaka- (most/-est)
The Philippines is the most beautiful.
Pinakamaganda ang Pilipinas.

Intensive
The Philippines is very beautiful.
Napakaganda ng Pilipinas.
Ang ganda-ganda ng Pilipinas.
Magandang maganda ang Pilipinas.
Sobrang ganda ng Pilipinas.

PART 10 The Body

91 **Masakit, Aray!** (It) Hurts/Ouch!

Ouch! It hurts.
Aray! Masakit.

Does it hurt?
Masakit ba?

Where does it hurt?/Which part hurts?
Saan ang masakit?

This hurts./(It is) very painful!
Masakit ito./Masyadong masakit!

It does not hurt anymore.
Hindi na masakit.

katawan body
ulo head
mukha face
mata eyes
ilong nose
bibig mouth
tenga ears
leeg neck
dibdib chest
balikat shoulders
braso arm
mga braso arms
kamay hand
mga kamay hands

daliri finger
mga daliri fingers
baywang or **bewang** waist
binti leg
mga binti legs
paa foot
mga paa feet
likod back

My body is sore.
Masakit ang katawan ko.

My head is aching.
Masakit ang ulo ko.

92 **Pakiramdam** Feeling

namamaga swollen
nahihilo dizzy
nasusuka nauseous
nauuhaw thirsty
nagtatae diarrhea
sakit ailment or sickness
ubo cough
sipon cold
lagnat fever
sugat wound

How are you feeling?
Kumusta ang pakiramdam mo?

I am not feeling well.
Masama ang pakiramdam ko.

Are you still not feeling well?
Masama pa ba ang pakiramdam mo?

I am feeling better now.
Mabuti na ang pakiramdam ko.

My eyes are swollen.
Namamaga ang mata ko.

I am getting dizzy because it is too hot today.
Nahihilo ako dahil masyadong mainit ngayon.

I am nauseous.
Nasusuka ako.

Martin is thirsty.
Nauuhaw si Martin.

I have diarrhea.
Nagtatae ako.

I have (a) cough, cold, and fever.
May ubo, sipon, at lagnat ako.

I am sick.
May sakit ako.

I have a wound.
May sugat ako.

93 Pasensya Na My Apologies

My apologies to you.
Pasensya ka na.

Sorry for the inconvenience.
Pasensya na sa abala.

Sorry, but I have to go.
Pasensya na pero kailangan ko nang umalis.

Sorry, I am not feeling well.
Pasensya na, masama ang pakiramdam ko.

Sorry, I cannot make it.
Pasensya na, hindi ako puwede.

Sorry, I need to leave early.
Pasensya na, kailangan ko umalis ng maaga.

94 Gamot Medicine

I need medicine.
Kailangan ko ng gamot.

Do you have medicine for diarrhea?
May gamot ka ba para sa nagtatae?

Buy (some) medicine at the pharmacy.
Bumili ka ng gamot sa botika.

You need to buy some medicine.
Kailangan mong bumili ng gamot.

tulungan to help
tinulungan helped
tinutulungan helping
tutulungan will help

Can you help me?
Puwede mo ba ako tulungan?

Do you need help?
Kailangan mo ba ng tulong?

I need your help.
Kailangan ko ng tulong mo.

Help me.
Tulungan mo ako.

Okay, I will help you.
Sige, tutulungan kita.

Thank you for the help.
Salamat sa tulong.

96 **Magaling** Healed/Well/Recovered from Illness

I have recovered (from the illness)./I am already well.
Magaling na ako.

Are you well?
Magaling ka na ba?

It is good to hear that you are feeling better.
Mabuti at magaling ka na.

My wound has healed.
Magaling na ang sugat ko.

The wound on my head has healed.
Magaling na ang sugat ko sa ulo.

97 **Malungkot** Sad
Matuwa Glad/Happy

I am feeling sad.
Nalulungkot ako.

I am glad.
Natutuwa ako.

Why are you sad?
Bakit ka malungkot?

Are you happy?
Natutuwa ka ba?/Masaya ka ba?

I am sad because our vacation is over.
Malungkot ako dahil tapos na ang bakasyon namin.

Are you sad that I am leaving?
Malungkot ka ba na aalis na ako?

Yes, I am sad too. I will miss you.
Oo malungkot din ako. Mamimiss kita.

I am glad to have met you.
Natutuwa ako at nakilala kita.

I am happy to hear the good news.
Natutuwa ako sa magandang balita.

98 **Balik** Come Back

bumalik come back, came back
bumabalik coming back
babalik will come back

Please come back (soon).
Bumalik ka ha.

I will come back.
Babalik ako.

Are you coming back?
Bumabalik ka ba?

When will you come back?
Kailan ka babalik?

I will come back next year.
Babalik ako sa susunod na taon.

99 **Dala** Bring

magdala bring
nagdala brought
nagdadala bringing
magdadala/dadalhin will bring

What do you have there?/What are you bringing?
Anong dala mo?

Bring some of these.
Magdala ka ng mga ito.

I will bring (back) some souvenirs for my co-workers.
Magdadala ako ng mga pasalubong para sa mga katrabaho ko.

What are you bringing?/What will you bring?
Anong dadalhin mo?

I will bring some friends.
Magdadala ako ng mga kaibigan.

maalaala/maalala to remember
naalaala/naalala remembered
naaalaala/naaalala remember
maaalaala/maaalala will remember

I have good memories here in the Philippines.
Maganda ang mga alaala ko dito sa Pilipinas.

You are the only memory that I have from the Philippines.
Ikaw lang ang alaala na mayroon ako sa Pilipinas.

A lot of good memories.
Maraming magagandang alaala.

I remembered you.
Naalala kita.

Do you remember me?
Naaalala mo ba ako?

Yes, I remember you.
Oo, naaalala kita.

Sorry, I cannot remember you.
Pasensya na, hindi kita maalala.

Do you remember when Chrys danced and sang at Ronald's party?
Naaalala mo ba noong sumayaw at kumanta si Chrys sa party ni Ronald?

I cannot remember when Jamie's birthday is.
Hindi ko maalala kung kailan ang bertdey ni Jamie.

I will remember this.
Maaalala ko ito.

I do not remember anything.
Wala akong maalala.

I remember the happy times with my new friends from the Philippines.
Naaalala ko ang mga masasayang oras kasama ang mga bago kong kaibigan sa Pilipinas.

I hope you remember us./I hope you do not forget us.
Sana maalala mo kami.

I hope you do not forget this.
Sana maalala mo ito.

Challenge

Kami ang mga awtor ng "Instant Tagalog". Sining at Tristan ang mga pangalan namin. **Sana** nagustuhan mo ang **librong** ito. **Siguradong** nakapunta ka sa magagandang tanawin at malilinis na mga tabing-dagat. Bumili ka **siguro** ng masasarap na pagkain at mga murang pasalubong. Sumakay ka rin **siguro** sa bangka o sa traysikel. **Sana** nagustuhan mo ang bakasyon sa Pilipinas. Maraming salamat sa pagbili ng **libro** namin at **sana** bumalik ka ulit sa Pilipinas sa susunod na buwan o taon.

Now you have reached the last part of the book and we hope that you understand what is written above. All the words, except the bolded ones, were covered in the book, so if you understood the paragraph then we have successfully accomplished our goal and the book has served its purpose. Challenge yourself and write simple sentences every day and a paragraph at the end of a week using the words presented in this book. As we discussed earlier, do not forget to say and share what you have written.

Additional Words:
sana I (we) hope
sigurado sure
libro book

APPENDIX

Seasons and Climate

The Philippines is known for its tropical weather. It only has two seasons: the wet (rainy) season and the dry season. All year long, the country tends to be hot even during the wet season. The average temperature is 25.5°C (77.9°F).

The expression, **Ang init!** which means "It's so hot!" is usually heard around the months of March until May, when the temperature can reach as high as 34.3°C (93.7°F). Baguio, Sagada and Tagaytay take pride in their cold weather; they are the most common destinations for people looking to cool down. In the cities, most people hang out at air-conditioned malls to escape the scorching hot weather.

Philippines is known to have many beautiful beaches. While Boracay is paradise for the party-goers and beach bums, nature lovers can explore seven thousand more islands, such as Bohol, Cebu's Bantayan and Malapascua Islands, Siargao, and Palawan.

The wet season usually starts around June and can last until October. During these months, monsoon rains and typhoons can be a big nuisance for travelers and tourists. Regardless, tourists still engage in water sports and road trips to provinces close to Manila like Batangas, Pampanga, and Laguna. It is recommended to have a contingency plan in case of bad weather.

Moving forward, the months of November until February should see a drop in temperature. **Ma-la-mig na!** "It is cold!" would usually be heard around these months. These are the months, when there is no rain and the temperature is perfect for foreign tourists.

Daily Expressions

	Informal	Polite
Hi, how are you?	**Hi, kumusta ka?**	**Hi, kamusta po kayo?**
I am fine. And you?	**Mabuti, ikaw?**	**Mabuti, kayo po?**
Where are you going?	**Saan ka pupunta?**	**Saan kayo pupunta?**
Take care.	**Ingat.**	**Ingat po (kayo).**
The weather is nice.	**Ang ganda ng panahon.**	**Ang ganda po ng panahon.**
Let us eat.	**Kain tayo.**	**Kain po tayo.**
Just a moment	**Sandali lang.**	**Sandali lang po.**
Thank you.	**Salamat.**	**Salamat po.**
You are welcome.	**Walang anuman.**	**Walang anuman po.**
How are you today?	**Kumusta ang araw mo?**	**Kumusta po ang araw ninyo?**
I love you.	**Mahal kita.**	**Mahal ko po kayo.**

Verb Conjugation

Filipino verbs have different classifications. The verbs used in this book have two: the **um** verb and the **mag** verb. Observe the pattern how they are conjugated to make the imperative, infinitive, completed, uncompleted and contemplated forms.

-UM-	Imperative/ Infinitive	Completed	Uncompleted	Contemplated
kain eat	kumain to eat	kumain ate	kumakain eat/eating	kakain will eat
punta go	pumunta to go	pumunta went	pumupunta go/going	pupunta will go
bili buy	bumili to buy	bumili bought	bumibili buy/buying	bibili will buy
gising wake up	gumising to wake up	gumising woke up	gumigising wake up/ waking up	gigising will wake up
sakay ride	sumakay to ride	sumakay rode	sumasakay ride/riding	sasakay will ride
baba go down	bumaba to go down	bumaba went down	bumababa go down/ going down	bababa will go down
takbo run	tumakbo to run	tumakbo ran	tumatakbo run/running	tatakbo will run
alis leave	umalis to leave	umalis left	umaalis leave/ leaving	aalis will leave
uwi go home	umuwi to go home	umuwi went home	umuuwi go home/ going home	uuwi will go home
inom drink	uminom to drink	uminom drank	umiinom drink/drinking	iinom will drink
akyat go up	umakyat to go up	umakyat went up	umaakyat go up/ going up	aakyat went up

MAG-	Imperative/ Infinitive	Completed	Uncompleted	Contemplated
bayad pay	magbayad to pay	nagbayad paid	nagbabayad pay/paying	magbabayad will pay
kita meet up	magkita to meet up	nagkita met up	nagkikita meet up/ meeting up	magkikita will meet up

sundo pick up	magsundo to pick up	nagsundo picked up	nagsusundo pick up/ picking up	magsusundo will pick up
lakad walk	maglakad to walk	naglakad walked	naglalakad walk/walking	maglalakad will walk
pahinga rest	magpahinga to rest	nagpahinga rested	nagpapahinga rest/resting	magpapahinga will rest

When you have mastered the conjugation of verbs, you are now ready to start constructing sentences, using the table below.

Verb	Subject Marker	Subject(s)—Person(s)' name(s), proper nouns Common noun	Object marker	Object
UM/ MAG completed/ uncompleted/ contemplated	si sina ang ang mga	(Common noun) ako siya sila kayo kami tayo ka	ng	

Question Words

Sino Who?
Who is he/she?
Sino siya?

Who is the tour guide?
Sino ang _tour guide_?

Ano What?
What is your son/daughter's name?
Ano ang pangalan ng anak mo?

What are we eating?/What is the food? (lit.)
Ano ang pagkain?

Saan Where?
Where are you going?
Saan ka pupunta?

Where did you come from?
Saan ka galing?

Nasaan Where?
Where are the students?
Nasaan ang mga estudyante?

Where is the CR?
Nasaan ang CR?

Ilan How many?
How many siblings do you have?
Ilan ang kapatid mo?

How many people are in the meeting room?
Ilan ang tao sa *meeting room*?

Magkano How much?
How much is the coffee?
Magkano ang kape?

How much is the massage?
Magkano ang masahe?

Kailan When?
When is your birthday?
Kailan ang bertdey mo?

Transportation List

eroplano airplane
kotse car
dyip jeep
jip jeepney
taksi taxi
traysikel tricycle
barko ship
bangka boat

Dictionary

A

about **tungkol sa**
above **sa itaas, sa ibabaw**
abroad **nasa ibang bansa**
address **tirahan**
admission **pagtanggap**
admission price **halaga ng tiket**
adult **nasa tamang gulang na**
advice **payo**
aeroplane **eroplano**
after **pagkatapos**
afternoon **hapon**
aftershave **losyon matapos mag-ahit**, *aftershave*
again **ulitin**
age **edad**
air **hangin** *ha-ng-in*
air-conditioning **erkon**
air mattress **kutson, kutsong de hangin**
airmail **sulat**
airplane **eroplano**
airport **paliparan, erport**
aisle **daanan**
aisle seat **upuan na malapit sa daanan**
alarm **sirena**
alarm clock **orasan**
alcohol **alak**

all day **buong araw**
all the time **palagi, sa lahat ng oras**
always **palagi**
ambulance **ambulansiya**
American **Amerikano**
amount **presyo**
amusement park **liwasan, amusement park**
anger **galit**
animal **hayop**
ankle **bukong-bukong**
answer **sagot**
ant **langgam**
antique **antigo, luma**
apartment **paupahan**
apologies **paumanhin, patawad**
apple **mansanas**
April **Abril**
arrogant **hambog**
art **sining, arte**
art gallery **galering pansining**
August **Agosto**
aunt **tita**
Australian **Australyano/a**
automatic **awtomatiko**
autumn **taglagas**
awake **gising**

B

baby **bata, batang paslit, sanggol**

baby food **pagkaing bata, pagkaing pangsanggol**

babysitter **tagapag-alaga ng bata**

back (part of body) **likuran**

back (rear) **likod**

bad (rotting) **sira, bulok**

bad (terrible) **masama**

baggage **bagahe**

baggage claim **kuhanan ng bagahe**

baker **panadero**

balcony **balkonahe**

ball **bola**

ballpoint pen **bolpen**

banana **saging**

bandage **benda**

bandaids **bandeyd**

bank (finance) **bangko**

bar (café) **kapehan**

bargain **tawad**

bath **ligo**

bath towel **tuwalya**

bathroom **paliguan, banyo**

battery **baterya**

beach **tabing-dagat**

beautiful **maganda**

because **dahil; kasi**

bed **kama**

bee **bubuyog**

beef **baka**

beer **serbesa**

begin **simula**

behind **sa likod**

belt **sinturon**

bicycle **bisikleta**

big **malaki**

bill, check **kuwenta, *bill***

billiards **bilyar**

billiard house **bilyaran**

bird **ibon**

birthday **kaarawan**

bitter **mapakla**

black **itim**

blue **asul**

blood **dugo**

boarding pass **pases para sa pagsakay, *boarding pass***

boat **bangka**

body **katawan**

bone **buto**

book **libro**

bottle **bote**

box **kahon**

box lunch **baunan**

boy **batang lalaki**

boyfriend **kasintahan**

brain **utak**

bread **tinapay**

breakfast **almusal**

bridge **tulay**
bright **maliwanag**
bronze **tanso**
brother **kapatid na lalaki**
brother-in-law **bayaw**
bruise **pasa**
building **gusali**
business **negosyo**
  ne-go-sho
but **pero**
butter **mantikilya**
butterfly **paruparo**

C
cabbage **repolyo**
cabin **kamarote,** *cabin*
cake **keyk**
call (phonecall) **tawag sa
  telepono**
call (to phone) **tatawag sa
  telepono**
called **tumawag**
camping **kamping**
can opener **abrelata**
cancel **kansela, di natuloy**
candle **kandila**
captain **kapitan**
car **kotse** *ko-che*
car documents **dokumento
  ng kotse, kasulatan ng
  kotse**
car seat (child's) **upuang
  pambata**

car trouble **sira ng kotse**
cardigan **kardigan, jaket**
careful **mag-ingat**
carpet **karpet**
cash **pera**
cash card **kas kard,** *cash
  card*
cash machine **makina ng
  pera, ATM**
casino **kasino, sugalan**
cat **pusa**
cave **kuweba**
celebrate **magdiwang,
  magsaya**
cellphone **selpon,**
  cellphone
center **gitna**
chair **upuan**
change **sukli**
change, swap **magpalit**
change (money) **magpalit
  ng pera**
change (trains) **magpalit
  ng tren, lumipat ng tren**
change the baby's diaper
  palitan ang dayaper
change the oil **palitan
  ang langis**
cheap **mura**
check (verb) **suriin,
  tingnan**
check in **magchek-in**
check out **magcheck-out**

checked luggage
  ipinalistang bagahe
cheek **pisngi**
cheese **keso**
chef **kusinero/a**
chess **ahedres**
chest **dibdib**
chicken **manok**
child **bata**
child (daughter, son) **anak**
chocolate **tsokolate**
choose **pumili**
chopsticks **chapsticks**
church **simbahan**
church service **misa sa
  simbahan**
Christmas **Pasko**
cigar/cigarette **sigarilyo**
cinema **sinehan**
circle **bilog**
circus **sirkus, sirko**
citizen **mamamayan**
city **lungsod**
clean **malinis**
cloud **ulap**
clock **orasan**
close **sarado**
clothes **damit**
clothes hanger *hanger* **ng
  damit**
clothes dryer **pantuyo ng
  damit**
cloud **ulap**

cloudy **maulap**
coat (overcoat) **panlamig**
cockroach **ipis**
cocoa **cacao, kakaw,
  sikulate**
coconut milk **gata**
coffee **kape**
coin **barya**
cold (illness) **sipon**
cold (temperature)
  malamig
colleague **kasama sa
  trabaho, katrabaho**
color **kulay**
comb **suklay**
come here **halika**
complaint **reklamo**
completely **lubos**
compliment **papuri**
concert **konsiyerto**
concert hall **bulwagang
  pangkonsiyerto**
congratulations **binabati
  kita, pagbati**
contact lens **kontak** *lens*
cook (person) **kusinera** (*f*),
  kusinero (*m*)
corn **mais**
cotton **bulak**
country **bansa**
cow **baka**
crab **alimango**
crazy **baliw**

crowded **matao**
cup **tasa**
curtain **kurtina**

D

dairy products **produktong gatas**
daily **araw-araw**
damage **pinsala**
dance **sayaw**
dandruff **balakubak**
danger **panganib**
dangerous **mapanganib; delikado**
dark **madilim**
date **petsa**
date of birth **araw ng kapanganakan**
daughter **anak na babae**
day **araw**
day after tomorrow **sa makalawa**
day before yesterday **kamakalawa**
dead **patay**
deaf **bingi**
death **kamatayan**
debt **utang**
December **Disyembre**
declare (customs) **magdeklara**
deep **malalim**

deep-sea diving **pagsisid sa malalim na dagat**
deliver **ipadala**
dentist **dentista**
departure **alis**
deposit (in bank) **deposito sa bangko**
deposit (for safekeeping) **patago**
desert **disyerto**
dessert **panghimagas**
diabetic **may diyabetis**
diarrhea **nagtatae**
dictionary **diksyunaryo**
diesel oil **disel**
diet **pagkain sa araw-araw, diyeta**
difficult **mahirap**
dining room **silid kainan**
dining table **hapag kainan**
dinner (meal) **hapunan**
direct flight **tuwirang paglipad, *direct flight***
directly **diretso, tuwiran**
dirt **dumi**
dirty **marumi**
disabled **may kapansanan**
discount **bawas sa presyo, diskwento, tawad**
disease **sakit**
distilled water **distiladong tubig**

disturb **istorbo, gambala**

disturbance **kaguluhan, gulo**

dive **magdive, sisid**

diving **magdiving, pagsisid**

diving board **daybing bord, *diving board***

diving gear **gamit pang-dive, gamit pagsisid**

divorced **diborsiyado/a, hiwalay**

dizzy **nahihilo, hilo, pagkahilo**

doctor **manggagamot**

dog **aso**

dollar **dolyar**

door **pinto**

draw, to **gumuhit**

dream **panaginip** *pa-na-gi-nop*

dress **damit**

drink (noun) **inumin**

drive, to **magmaneho**

driver **drayber**

drizzle **ambon**

drugstore **butika**

drunk **lasing**

dry **tuyo**

duck **pato**

dust **alikabok**

E

each **bawat**

eagle **agila**

ear **tainga**

ear drops **gamot para sa tainga**

earache **pananakit ng tainga**

early **maaga**

earrings **hikaw**

earth **lupa**

earthenware **gawa sa lupa, palayok, pinalayok**

earthquake **lindol**

east **silangan**

easy **madali**

eat, to **kumain**

economy class **ekonomi klas**

eczema **eksema**

eel **palos, balila**

egg **itlog**

eggplant **talong**

elbow **siko**

electric **de-kuryente**

electric fan **bentilador, elektrik fan**

electricity **kuryente**

elephant **elepante**

embassy **embahada**

embrace, to **yakapin**

embroidery **pagboborda**

emergency brake **prenong pangkagipitan**

emergency exit **labasang pangkagipitan, labasang pang-emergency**

empty **walang laman**

entrance **pasukan**

evening **gabi**

everything **lahat**

example **halimbawa**

exit **labasan**

expensive **mahal**

eye **mata**

eyebrow **kilay**

eyeglasses **salamin sa mata**

F

fabric **tela**

face **mukha**

Facebook **Peysbuk, *Facebook***

fall (autumn) **taglagas**

fall (verb) **bumagsak**

fake **peke**

family **pamilya**

famous **kilalang-kilala, sikat**

fan **pamaypay**

far **malayo**

fare **pamasahe**

fashion **uso**

fast **mabilis, madali**

father **tatay**

father-in-law **biyenan na lalaki**

February **Pebrero**

fee **bayad**

feel **hawakan, hipuin**

feel like **nararamdaman**

feeling **pakiramdam**

female **babae**

fence **bakod**

ferry **barko, feri**

fever **lagnat**

festival **pagdiriwang; pista**

fiancé **mapapangasawa, nobyo**

fiancée **mapapangasawa, nobya**

file (computer) **file sa kompyuter**

fill **punuin, lagyan**

fill out (form) **sagutan**

film (cinema) **pelikula**

find, to **hanapin**

fine (good) **mabuti**

fine (punishment) **multa**

fire **apoy; sunog**

fire alarm **hudyat ng apoy, alarma sa sunog**

fire department **kagawaran sa sunog**

fire escape **labasan kapag may sunog**

fire extinguisher **pamatay ng sunog, *fire extinguisher***

fireman **bumbero**
firework **paputok**
first **una**
first class **primera klase**
fish **isda**
fish sauce **patis**
fishing rod **pamingwit**
fitting room **silid sukatan**
fix, to (repair) **ayusin**
flag **bandila**
flash (camera) **ilaw ng kamera**
flavor **lasa**
flavoring **pampalasa**
flight **paglipad, lipad**
flight number **lipad numero**
flood **baha**
floor (level) **palapag**
floor (ground) **sahig**
flour **arina**
flower **bulaklak**
flu **trangkaso**
fly (insect) **langaw**
fly, to **lumipad**
fog **ulap**, *fog*
foggy **malabo, maulap**
folklore **kuwentong bayan**
follow **sumunod**
food (groceries) **pagkain, groseri**
food (meal) **agahan, tanghalian, hapunan, ulam**
food court **kainan**

food poisoning **nalason sa pagkain**
foot **paa**
foot brake **preno sa paanan**
forbidden **ipinagbabawal**
forehead **noo**
foreign **banyaga, dayuhan**
foreigner **dayuhan**
forest **gubat**
forget, to **limutin**
forgive, to **magpatawad**
fork **tinidor**
formal dress **pormal na damit**
forward (letter) **ipadala**
fountain **fawnteyn**, *fountain*
free of charge **libre**
free (unoccupied) **bakante, walang nakatira**
free time **libreng oras**
French fries **pritong patatas, prens prays**, *French fries*
frequent **madalas**
fresh **sariwa**
Friday **Biyernes**
fried **prito**
friend **kaibigan**
friendly **palakaibigan**
frightened **takot, natatakot**
fringe (hair) **nakalugay**
from **mula**
front **harap**
frozen **nagyelo**

fruit **prutas**
frying pan **kawali**
full **puno**
full (after eating) **busog**
fun, to have **magsaya**
funeral **libing, paglilibing**
funny **nakakatawa**

G
gallery **galeri**
gamble **sugal**
game **laro**
garbage **basura**
garbage can **basurahan**
garden **hardin**
garlic **bawang**
garment **damit**
gasoline **gasolina**
gasoline station **gasolinahan**
gate **geyt, labasan**
gather, to **magtipon**
gear (car) **kambiyo**
gem **hiyas, mamahaling bato**
gender **kasarian**
genuine **tunay**
get, receive **makatanggap**
get off (disembark) **bumaba**
get on (embark) **sumakay**
get up (from bed) **bumangon**
gift **regalo**
ginger **luya**
girl **batang babae**

girlfriend **kasintahang babae, nobya**
give, to **magbigay**
given name **pangalan**
glass (for drinking) **baso**
glasses, spectacles **salamin**
gliding **mag-glayding, gliding**
gloves **guwantes**
glue **pandikit**
go, to **pumunta**
go along **sumabay**
go back **bumalik**
go for a walk **maglakad**
go home **umuwi**
go out **lumabas**
go to bed **matulog**
go up, climb **umakyat**
goat **kambing**
gold **ginto**
golf **golp, golf**
golf course **laruan ng golp, golf course**
good **mabuti**
good afternoon **magandang hapon**
good evening/night **magandang gabi**
good morning **magandang umaga**
goodbye **paalam**
goose **gansa**
gram **gramo**

granddaughter **apong babae**

grandfather **lolo**

grandmother **lola**

grandson **apong lalaki**

grape **ubas**

grape juice **katas ng ubas,** *grape juice*

grass **damo**

grave **malubha, malala, puntod**

gray **kulay-abo, abuhin,** *grey*

gray-haired **ubanin, maputing buhok**

greasy **malangis**

great, impressive **magaling**

green **berde**

greet, to **batiin**

guest **bisita**

guide (person) **gabay**

guided tour **pamamasyal na may gabay,** *guided tour*

guilty **may sala, may kasalanan**

gynecologist **hinekologo, OB**

H

hair **buhok**

hairbrush **suklay,** *brush*

haircut **magpagupit**

hairdresser **taga-ayos ng buhok**

hairdryer **pantuyo ng buhok**

hairspray **pangwisik ng buhok,** *spray* **sa buhok**

hairstyle **istilo ng buhok**

half **kalahati**

half full **kalahati ang laman**

hammer **martilyo**

hand **kamay**

hand brake **kambiyo**

hand luggage **bagaheng bitbit**

hand towel **tuwalyang pangkamay**

handkerchief **panyo, panyolito**

handmade **gawa sa kamay**

handsome **guwapo** *gwa-po*

happy **maligaya**

Happy Birthday **Maligayang Kaarawan**

hard, difficult **mahirap**

hard, solid **matigas**

hardware store **tindahan ng kagamitang** *metal,* *hardware*

hat **sumbrero**

hay fever **sipong may lagnat**

head **ulo**

headache **sakit ng ulo**

headlights **hedlayt, ilaw sa harapan**

health food shop **tindahan ng pagkaing**

masustansiya, tindahan
ng pagkaing
pangkalusugan

healthy **malusog**

hear **marinig**

hearing aid **tulong sa
pandinig**

heart **puso**

heart attack **atake sa puso**

heat **init**

heater **pampainit**

heavy **mabigat**

heel (of foot) **sakong**

heel (of shoe) **takong**

hello **helo, halo, hoy**

help **tulong**

helping (of food) **pagkain**

hem **tupi, lupi, laylayan**

herbal tea **tsaang herbal**

here **dito, narito**

hide, to **magtago**

high **mataas**

high chair **silyang may
sandalan, silyang
pambata**

high tide **paglaki ng tubig,
mataas ang alon**

highway **hi-way**

hiking **mahabang
paglalakbay, hayking,
mag-hiking**

hiking boots **panghayking
na sapatos, sapatos sa**

paglalakbay, **botas na
panghiking**

hill **burol**

hips **balakang**

hire **umupa, arkila**

hitchhike **makisakay**

hobby **libangan, hilig**

hold, to **hawakan**

hole **butas**

holiday (festival) **pista**

holiday (vacation) **bakasyon**
ba-ka-shon

Holy Week **Mahal na Araw**

home **tahanan**

homesick **sabik sa pag-uwi,
nangungulila**

honest **matapat**

horse **kabayo**

honey **pulut-pukyutan,
hani**

horizontal **pahalang,
pahiga**

horrible **kakila-kilabot**

horse **kabayo**

hospital **ospital**

hot (spicy) **maanghang**

hot (temperature) **mainit**

hot spring **mainit na bukal**

hot-water bottle **boteng
pangmainit na tubig**

hotel **otel**

hour **oras**

house **bahay**

how **paano**
How far? **Gaano kalayo? Malayo ba?**
How long? **Gaano katagal? Matagal ba?**
How many? **Ilan? Gaano karami?**
How much? **Magkano? Ano ang presyo?**
huge **malaki**
hungry **gutom**
hurry **bilisan**
hurt, to **saktan**
husband **asawang lalaki**
hut **kubo**

I

ice **yelo**
ice cream **sorbetes**
ice cubes **yelong kubiko**
ice-skating **iskeyting sa yelo**, *ice skating*
iced **may yelo**
idea **ideya**
identification (card) **ID, kard pagkakakilanlan, identipikasyon kard**
identify **kilalanin, tukuyin**
ignition key **susi sa ignisyon**
if **kung**
ill, sick **may sakit**
illness **sakit**

imagine **ilarawan sa sarili, isipin**
immediately **agad-agad, dali-dali**
impolite **bastos**
import duty **buwis sa pag-angkat**
important **mahalaga, importante**
impossible **hindi maaari, imposible**
improve **pagbutihin, ayusin**
in **nasa, sa**
in the evening **sa gabi**
in the morning **sa umaga**
in-laws **partido ng asawa, pamilya ng asawa**
included **kasama, kalahok, kabilang**
including **pagkakasama, pagkakalahok, pati**
indicate **magturo, magtukoy, tukuyin, isali**
indicator (car) **indikador ng kotse, indiykator**
indigestion **hindi natunawan, impatso**
inexpensive **hindi mahal, mura**
infection **impeksiyon**
infectious **nakahahawa**
inflammation **pamamaga**
information **impormasyon**

information office **tanggapan/opisina pang-impormasyon**
injection **iniksiyon, pagturok**
injured **nasaktan, nasugatan**
inner tube **panloob na tubo**
innocent **walang-sala, inosente**
insect **insekto**
inside **sa loob**
international **pandaigdig**
Internet café **Internet Kafe**
interpreter **tagapagsalin, tagapagpaliwanag**
intersection **krosing, interseksyon**
interested **interesado**
intestine **bituka**
island **isla**

J

jack (for car) **dyak, kalso**
jacket **jaket, dyaket**
jackfruit **langka**
jam **halaya**
January **Enero**
jeans **pantalon**
jellyfish **dikya**
jeweler **alahero, mag-aalahas**
jewelry **alahas**

job **trabaho**
joke **biro**
journey **paglalakbay**
July **Hulyo**
jump, to **tumalon**
June **Hunyo**

K

kerosene **gas, gaas**
key **susi**
key (on a keyboard) **ki**
keyboard **kibord**
kidney **bato**
kilogram **kilo**
kilometer **kilometro**
kind (nice) **mabait**
king **hari**
kiss **halik**
kitchen **kusina**
knee **tuhod**
knife **kutsilyo**
knit **gantsilyo**
knock, to **kumatok**
know **malaman, mabatid**

L

lace (fabric) **leys**
laces (for shoes) **tali ng sapatos**
ladder **hagdan**
lake **lawa**
lamb **batang tupa**
lamp **ilawan, lampara**

land **lupa**
land, to (plane) **lumapag**
language **wika, lengguwahe**
laptop **laptap**
large **malaki**
last **huli**
last day **huling araw**
last month **huling buwan**
last night **kagabi**
last week **huling linggo**
last year **huling taon**
late **nahuli, naantala**
later **mamaya**
laugh **tawa, tumawa, pagtawa**
launderette **londri, palabahan**
laundry **labahan**
lawyer **abogado**
laxative *laxative*, **gamot sa constipasyon**
lazy **tamad**
leaf **dahon**
leather goods **gawa sa balat**
leave **umalis, pag-alis**
left (direction) **kaliwa**
left behind **naiwan**
leg **paa**
leggings **legings, pulinas**
leisure **pahinga, pagllilibang**
lemon **dayap, limon**
lend **magpahiram, hiram, pahiram**

lens (camera) **lente ng kamera**
less **kulang, kaunti, mas maliit**
lesson **aralin**
letter **sulat**
lettuce **litsugas**
library **aklatan**
lice **kuto**
license **lisensiya, permiso**
lie (lying) **nagsisinungaling, liar-sinungaling**
lie (falsehood) **hindi totoo, walang katotohanan**
lie down **nakahiga, humiga**
lift (in car) **makisakay**
light **ilaw**
light (not heavy) **magaan**
lightning **kidlat**
like (verb) **magkagusto, maibigan, gusto**
like that **ganyan**
like this **ganito**
line (queue) **pila**
lip **labi**
liquor **alak**
liquor store **tindahan ng alak**
listen, to **makinig**
literature **literatura, panitikan**
little (amount) **kaunti, maliit na halaga**

little (small) **maliit**
live (alive) **buhay**
live (verb) **mabuhay, mamuhay, nakatira**
livelihood **hanapbuhay**
liver **atay**
lizard **butiki**
lobster **ulang**
local **lokal**
lock, to **isara**
log off **maglog out**
log on **maglog in**
long **mahaba**
long-distance call **mag-long distance**
lost **nawawala**
love **pag-ibig**
love, to **umibig**
low **mababa**
luggage **bagahe**
lunch **tanghalian**
lung **baga**

M

machine **makina**
magazine **magasin**
maid **katulong**
maiden **dalaga**
make, to **gumawa**
man/male **lalaki**
mango **mangga**
many **marami**
map **mapa**

market **palengke**
married **kasal na, may asawa na**
mask **maskara**
March **Marso**
mass **misa, mga tao**
massage **masahe**
mat **banig**
May **Mayo**
meat **karne**
medicine **gamot**
meet, to **magtagpo; magkita**
menu **menyu**
message **mensahe**
meter (in taxi) **metro ng taksi**
middle **gitna**
midnight **hatinggabi**
mild (not spicy) **hindi maanghang**
mild (not severe) **hindi malala**
milk **gatas**
milkfish **bangus**
mineral water **tubig na mineral**
mirror **salamin**
missing (lost person) **nawawala**
mistake **kamalian, pagkakamali**
mistaken **nagkakamali**

misunderstanding **hindi pagkakaunawaan**
mix, to **maghalo**
mold **amag**
Monday **Lunes**
money **pera**
monkey **unggoy**
moon/month **buwan** *bwan*
morning **umaga**
mosquito **lamok**
mother **nanay**
mother-in-law **biyenan na babae**
motorbike **motorsiklo**
motorboat **bangkang de motor**
mountain **bundok**
mountain range **bulubundukin**
mouse **daga**
mouth **bibig**
movie **pelikula**
much **marami**
music **musika**

N

nail (finger) **kuko**
nail (metal) **pako**
nail file **kikil ng kuko**
name **pangalan**
nationality **pagkamamamayan, nasyonalidad**

natural **likas**
nature **kalikasan**
nauseous **naduduwal, nahihilo**
near **malapit**
nearby **malapit lang**
necessary **kailangan**
neck **leeg**
necklace **kuwintas**
necktie **kurbata**
negative (photo) **negatibo, *negative film***
neighbor **kapitabahay**
nephew **pamangking lalaki**
new **bago**
news **balita**
New Year **Bagong Taon**
news stand **tindahan ng diyaryo**
newspaper **pahayagan, peryodiko**
next **susunod**
next month **susunod na buwan** *su-su-nod na bwan*
next week **susunod na linggo**
next year **susunod na taon**
new **bago**
news **balita**
nice (person) **mabait na tao, mabuting tao**
nice (pleasant) **maaliwalas, kaaya-aya, maganda**

niece **pamangking babae**
night **gabi**
noisy **maingay**
north **hilaga**
nose **ilong**
November **Nobyembre**
now **ngayon**
numb **manhid**
number **bilang, numero**

O

obey, to **sumunod**
occupation **hanapbuhay,**
  trabaho
ocean **karagatan**
October **Oktubre**
off (gone bad) **nasira**
off (turned off) **pinatay**
  (ilaw)
offer **alok**
office **opisina**
often **madalas**
oil **langis**
ointment **oynment,**
  pamahid
okay **okey lang**
old (age) **matanda**
old **luma**
once **isang beses**
onion **sibuyas**
open **bukas**
or **o**
order, to **mag-utos**

order something, to **mag-**
  order
ouch **aray**
outside **sa labas**
own, to **mag-ari**
oyster **talaba**

P

pack, to **magbalot**
package **pakete**
paid **bayad**
painful **masakit**
paint **pintura**
paint, to **magpinta**
pants **pantalon**
paper **papel**
parents **mga magulang**
park **parke**
park, to **gumarahe**
parking **paradahan**
passport **pasaporte**
pay, to **magbayad**
payment **kabayaran**
peace **kapayapaan**
peaceful **mapayapa**
peak, summit **tuktok**
peanut **mani**
pearl **perlas**
pedestrian **tawiran**
pencil **lapis**
people **mga tao**
pepper, black **paminta**
pepper, chili **siling labuyo**

perfume **pabango**
perhaps, maybe **marahil**
perhaps, probably
  malamang
period (menstruation) **regla**
permit, to allow **pumayag**
person **tao**
perspire, to **magpapawis**
pharmacy **botika**
photograph **larawan**
pick-up (someone) **sunduin**
pick-up, lift **buhatin**
piece **piraso**
pig **baboy**
pillow **unan**
pineapple **pinya**
place **lugar**
plan **balak, plano**
plan, to **magbalak,
  magplano**
plane **eroplano**
plant **halaman**
plant, to **magtanim**
plastic **plastik**
plate **plato**
play, to **maglaro**
pocket **bulsa**
poisonous **nakakalason**
policeman **pulis**
poor **mahirap**
popular **sikat**
potato **patatas**
pour, to **ibuhos**

powerful **malakas,
  makapangyarihan**
prawn **sugpo**
pray, to **magdasal**
pregnant **buntis**
prepare, to **maghanda**
private **pribado**
probably **marahil, siguro**
problem **problema**
promise, to **mangako**
pull, to **hilahin**
push, to **itulak**
put on (clothes) **magdamit,
  magbihis**

Q

question **tanong**
queue, line **pila**
queue, to line up **pumila**
quick **mabilis**
quiet **tahimik**

R

railroad **riles**
rain **ulan**
rainbow **bahaghari**
rarely **bihira**
rat **daga**
raw, uncooked **hilaw**
reach, get to **makarating**
read, to **magbasa**
ready, to get **maghanda**
receipt **resibo**

receive, to **tumanggap**
red **pula**
reduce, to **magbawas**
refuse, to **tumanggi**
rent **renta, upa**
rent, to **umupa**
repair **ayos**
replace, to **palitan**
restroom **C.R.**
respect, to **igalang**
response **sagot**
rest, to relax **magpahinga**
return, go back **bumalik**
return, give back **ibalik**
rice (uncooked) **bigas**
rice (cooked) **kanin**
rich **mayaman**
ride, to **sumakay**
right (direction) **kanan**
ring **singsing**
ripe **hinog**
river **ilog**
road **kalye**
rock **bato**
room **kwarto**
rotten **bulok**
rubber **goma**
run, to **tumakbo**

S
sad **malungkot**
safe **ligtas**
salt **asin**

salty **maalat**
sauce **sawsawan**
say goodbye **magpaalam**
say hello **mangumusta**
say thank you
  magpasalamat
school **paaralan**
scissors **gunting**
sea **dagat**
seafood **pagkaing dagat**
seashore **dalampasigan**
season **panahon**
seat **upuan**
see, to **tingnan**
sell, to **magtinda**
send, to **magpadala**
seldom **bihira**
select, to **pumili**
September **Setyembre**
shark **pating**
sharp **matalim**
sheep **tupa**
ship **barko**
shirt **damit pantaas**
shoes **sapatos**
shoulder **balikat**
show **palabas**
shop, to **mamili**
short (length) **maikli**
short (height) **mababa**
store **tindahan**
shout, to **sumigaw**
shrimp **hipon**

sibling (as in brother/sister) **kapatid**
silver **pilak**
sing **awit**
sing, to **kumanta**
sister-in-law **hipag**
sit, to **umupo**
skin **balat**
skirt **palda**
sky **himpapawid**
sleep, to **matulog**
sleepy **inaantok**
slow **mabagal**
smile, to **ngumiti**
smooth (surface) **makinis**
snake **ahas**
soap **sabon**
son **anak na lalaki**
song **kanta**
soup **sabaw**
sour **maasim**
south **timog**
soy sauce **toyo**
speak, to **magsalita**
spend, to **gumastos**
spicy **maanghang**
spider **gagamba**
spoiled (food) **panis**
spoon **kutsara**
spouse **asawa**
spring (season) **tagsibol**
spring **bukal**
squid **pusit**

stand, to **tumayo**
stomach **tiyan**
straight **diretso**
sugar **asukal**
summer **tag-init**
sun **araw**
surname **apelyido**
stop, to **tumigil**
street **kalye**
storm **bagyo**
student **estudyante**
suck, to **sipsipin**
sugar **asukal**
suitcase **maleta**
summer **tag-araw**
sunny **maaraw**
swallow, to **lunukin**
sweat **pawis**
sweet **matamis**
swim, to **lumangoy**

T
table **lamesa, mesa**
take care of, to **mag-alaga**
take off (clothes) **maghubad**
talk, to **mag-usap**
tall **mataas, matangkad**
taste **lasa**
taste, to **lashaan**
tea **tsaa**
teach, to **magturo**
teacher **guro**

tears **luha**
television **telebisyon**
temperature **temperatura**
theater **sinehan, teatro**
thick **makapal**
thigh **hita**
thin **payat; manipis**
thing **bagay**
thirsty **nauuhaw**
throat **lalamunan**
thunder **kulog**
ticket **tiket**
tidy **malinis**
tie **kurbata**
time **oras**
toilet **palikuran; banyo**
tomato **kamatis**
tomorrow **bukas**
tongue **dila**
tonight **mamayang gabi**
tooth **ngipin**
toothbrush **sipilyo**
tourist **turista**
toy **laruan**
traffic **trapik**
train **tren**
tree **puno**
turn off, to **patayin**
turn on, to **buksan**
turtle **pagong**
typhoon **bagyo**

U

ugly **pangit**
umbrella **payong**
uncle **tiyo; tito**
undershirt **sando**
urinate **umihi**
use, to **gamitin**

V

vacant **ba-kan-te**
vacation **bakasyon**
vaccinate **pagbakuna, bakunahan**
valid **tunay, totoo, may bisa**
valley **lambak**
value **halaga**
valuable **mahalaga, mamahalin**
valuables **mga mahalagang bagay**
vase **plorera**
vegetable **gulay**
vegetarian **gulay lamang ang kinakain**
vegetable **gulay**
vending machine **makinang nagtitinda, makinang tindahan, vendo** *machine*
venomous **makamandag**
via **sa pamamagitan ng**
video **bidyo**
view **tanawin**

village **nayon, baryo**
vinegar **suka**
virgin **birhen**
visa **bisa,** *visa*
visit, to **dalawin; bisitahin**
visitor **bisita**
voice **boses**
volcano **bulkan**
volleyball **balibol,** *volleyball*
vomit, to **magsuka**

W

wait for **maghintay**
waiter **serbidor, weyter**
waiting room **silid hintayan**
waitress **serbidora, weytress**
wake up **gumising**
walk, to **maglakad**
walk (noun) **lakad**
walk (verb) **lumakad**
walking stick **tungkod**
wall **bakod, pader**
wallet **pitaka**
wardrobe **aparador**
warm **medyo mainit**
warn **babala, paalaala, bigyan ng babala**
warning **pagbabala, pagpapaalaala, babala** (n)
wash, to **maghugas**
washing line **sampayan**

washing machine **makinang panlaba,** *washing machine*
wasp **putakti**
watch, to **manood**
watch **manood, magbantay, magmasid**
water **tubig**
water-skiing **pag-iski sa tubig, mag-waterski**
waterfall **talon**
waterproof **hindi nababasa**
wave **alon**
wave, to **kumaway**
way (direction) **daan**
way (method) **paraan**
we **kami, tayo**
weak **mahina**
wear **suot, magsuot**
wealthy **mayaman**
weather **panahon**
weather forecast **magiging panahon, magiging klima, lagay ng panahon**
wedding **kasalan**
Wednesday **Miyerkules**
week **linggo**
weekday **araw ng linggo, araw na may pasok**
weekend **Sabado at Linggo, araw na walang pasok**
weigh **timbang**

weigh out **ayusin sa timbang**
welcome **maligayang pagdating**
well (good) **mabuti**
well-cooked (well-done) **lutong-luto**
west **kanluran**
wet **basa**
wetsuit **witsut, damit pantubig, *wetsuit***
what **ano**
wheel **gulong**
wheelchair **upuang may gulong, *wheelchair***
when **kailan** *kay-lan*
which **alin**
while **habang**
white **puti**
white wine **puting alak, puting *wine***
who **sino**
whose **kanino**
wheel **gulong**
why **bakit**
win, to **manalo**
wind **hangin**
window **bintana**
wine **alak**
wing **pakpak**
winner **panalo**
winter **taglamig**
wipe, to **punasan**

woman/women **babae/mga babae**
wood **kahoy**
work **trabaho**
work, to **magtrabaho**
wound **sugat**
wrap, to **balutin**
wrench, spanner **liyabe, panghigpit**
wrist **pulso**
write, to **sumulat**
write down **isulat**
writing pad/paper **sulatang pad/papel**
wrong **mali**

X
x-ray **eksrey, *x-ray***

Y
yarn **sinulid**
year **taon**
yell, to **sumigaw**
year **taon**
yellow **dilaw**
yes **oo**
yes please **oo salamat**
yesterday **kahapon**
you **ikaw**
young **bata**
youth hostel **tirahan pangkabataan**

About Tuttle Story
"Books to Span the East and West"

Our core mission at Tuttle Publishing is to create books which bring people together one page at a time. Tuttle was founded in 1832 in the small New England town of Rutland, Vermont (USA). Our fundamental values remain as strong today as they were then—to publish best-in-class books informing the English-speaking world about the countries and peoples of Asia. The world has become a smaller place today and Asia's economic, cultural and political influence has expanded, yet the need for meaningful dialogue and information about this diverse region has never been greater. Since 1948, Tuttle has been a leader in publishing books on the cultures, arts, cuisines, languages and literatures of Asia. Our authors and photographers have won numerous awards and Tuttle has published thousands of books on subjects ranging from martial arts to paper crafts. We welcome you to explore the wealth of information available on Asia at **www.tuttlepublishing.com**.

Published by Tuttle Publishing, an imprint of Periplus Editions (HK) Ltd.

www.tuttlepublishing.com

Copyright © 2016 Periplus Editions (HK) Ltd.

Library of Congress Control Number: 2016944517.

ISBN 978-0-8048-3941-9

First edition
20 19 18 17 16   5 4 3 2 1   1609CM
Printed in China

Distributed by

North America, Latin America & Europe
Tuttle Publishing
364 Innovation Drive,
North Clarendon,
VT 05759-9436, USA
Tel: 1 (802) 773 8930
Fax: 1 (802) 773 6993
info@tuttlepublishing.com
www.tuttlepublishing.com

Asia Pacific
Berkeley Books Pte Ltd
61 Tai Seng Avenue #02-12
Singapore 534167
Tel: (65) 6280 1330
Fax: (65) 6280 6290
inquiries@periplus.com.sg
www.periplus.com